This edition first published 2024
© 2024 One Golden Nugget

The right of the author to be identified as the author of this work has been asserted in accordance with the Copyright, Designs and Patents Act 1988.

All rights reserved. No part of this publication may be reproduced, stored in a retrieval system, or transmitted, in any form or by any means, electronic, mechanical, photocopying, recording or otherwise, except as permitted by the UK Copyright, Designs and Patents Act 1988, without the prior permission of the publisher.

Designations used by companies to distinguish their products are often claimed as trademarks. All brand names and product names used in this book are trade names, service marks, trademarks or registered trademarks of their respective owners. The publisher is not associated with any product or vendor mentioned in this book. This publication is designed to provide acurate and authoritive information in regard to the subject matter covered. It is sold on the understanding that the publisher is not engaged in rendering professional services. If professional advice or other expert assistance is required, the services of a competent professional should be sort.

As the publisher, we are proud to present this work on behalf of the authors. While we have taken every care to edit and review the content thoroughly, Errors and Omissions Excepted (E&OE), we cannot guarantee that the book is free from errors or omissions. We appreciate your understanding.

Editor-In-Chief: Greta Gard
Writer: Anna Gard
Researcher: Maxwell Preece
Designer: David Torres Mora

Registered office
7-8 Church St, Wimborne BH21 1JH

Published by One Golden Nugget
ISBN: 978-1-0687318-4-6

DO YOU HAVE A STORY TO SHARE?
BECOME A CO-AUTHOR
WWW.ONEGOLDENNUGGET.COM

HOW TO SURVIVE AND THRIVE
Podcast

LISTEN NOW

How to Survive and Thrive II

CONTENTS

Introduction	1
Rick Macci	6
Ian Fishwick	20
Mirela Sula	34
Darren Leigh	48
Let's Share Wisdom	60
Hacia Atherton	72
Kevin Hines	86
Dr. Akhtar Badshah	100
Dr. Amine Arezki	114
Let's Share Wisdom	128
Carla Berbary	140
Nick and Melissa Stehr	152
Cristian Caponi	168
John Attridge	182
Let's Share Wisdom	196
Gayatree Dipchan	208
Devon Harris	226
Volker Jaeckel	238
Abraham Charles	252
Let's Share Wisdom	266
Indira Nicole Persad	278
Mike Radoor	292
Chris Browne	304
Manny Ohonme	318
Let's Share Wisdom	332
Ellen Williams	341
Gratitude	343

How to Survive and Thrive II

INTRODUCTION

I never pictured myself as an elderly man, content with a quiet life of slippers and pipes. Yet I also never imagined the incredible journey I'd embark on—travelling the world, meeting extraordinary innovators and changemakers, and uncovering their powerful stories of perseverance and success. The first *Survive and Thrive* taught me a great deal about the indomitable human spirit. In those stories, I discovered profound truths—vulnerability as strength, the courage to reinvent oneself, and the importance of community in lifting each other up.

What truly stands out isn't just the victories but the courage to face failures, learn from them, and keep rising, no matter how many times it takes. Each story—whether about personal trauma, career reinvention, or navigating unexpected detours—demonstrates our incredible ability to adapt, grow, and turn adversity into opportunity. In this edition, I gained an even deeper appreciation for how people turn setbacks into stepping stones and how imagination and adaptability lead to innovation in every aspect of life.

Given my experience at Reebok, it's always a pleasure to interview people who share my passion for sports. This time, I had the privilege of speaking with two remarkable figures, like **Rick Macci**, coach to legends Venus and Serena Williams, and **Devon Harris** of the 1988 Olympic Jamaican bobsleigh team.

Though they come from vastly different sports, both men exemplify the same core values: relentless hard work and unwavering tenacity. Rick Macci's commitment to nurturing young talent and shaping tennis legends is nothing short of inspiring. His work with Venus and Serena Williams, in particular, stands as a testament to his ability to cultivate raw potential and push athletes to reach their fullest capabilities, regardless of the obstacles they face.

Devon's story showcases a different kind of resilience—one forged by breaking barriers and defying expectations. As a member of the iconic Jamaican bobsleigh team, he didn't just make history; he demonstrated that with determination, even the seemingly impossible can be achieved. Both Rick and Devon remind us that greatness is built on grit, perseverance, and the courage to push beyond comfort zones—a valuable lesson that resonates not only in sports but also in life.

As I approach my ninetieth year, it was a true pleasure to speak with one of the youngest contributors, **Cristian Caponi**, and witness someone at the dawn of what promises to be a remarkable entrepreneurial journey. Cristian's approach is dynamic and innovative, emblematic of his generation, yet his appreciation for timeless principles—like resilience, integrity, and hard work—bridges the gap between youthful ambition and seasoned wisdom. This blend of fresh vision and respect for experience fills me with confidence for the future, knowing that the next generation is not only prepared to build on what we've learned but also ready to forge their own unique path forward.

Social heroes are plentiful in *Survive and Thrive*, and the generosity to uplift others is best exemplified by **Dr. Akhtar Badshah**, whose organisation, Purpose Mindset, inspires both individuals and businesses to change the world. By guiding others to lead with intention and compassion, Akhtar shows that true success isn't solely defined by personal achievement but by the positive difference we make in the lives of others.

Manny Ohonme's story is both uplifting and thought-provoking, showing how seemingly small childhood events can leave a lasting impact, shaping one's attitude well into adulthood. He faced an inner struggle when deciding to leave the security and comfort of his executive role to pursue his passion—creating a charity dedicated to providing shoes for millions of children in need. His journey reflects the power of faith and the courage it takes to follow a calling for the greater good.

Mirela Sula has turned her painful life experiences into a powerful source of energy, driving her mission to help others overcome adversity. Through her work, she inspires people to persevere and carve their own paths to thriving—no matter the obstacles they face. Mirela's journey shows how personal struggles can be transformed into a force for good, empowering others to rise above their hardships and find strength in resilience.

Similarly, **Hacia Atherton** champions this cause by advocating for women in skilled trades. After facing discrimination herself, she now leads initiatives to open doors for women in industries traditionally dominated by men. Her advocacy goes beyond gender equality; Hacia understands that when women thrive, the entire economy benefits. These individuals are more than survivors—they are champions of change, using their personal hardships as a springboard to empower others and create lasting impact. Through their resilience, they inspire transformation and pave the way for future generations.

Indira Nicole Persad, a transformational leader with a vision for meaningful change, is focused on creating sustainable employment opportunities that uplift communities. With a collaborative approach, she guides business leaders in building resilient, people-centric workplaces. Equally passionate about empowering young women, she seeks to inspire them to embrace independence, understand their worth, and confidently pursue their ambitions in the business world. Through her work, Indira is shaping a future where professional success goes hand in hand with personal empowerment and social impact.

From a purely business perspective, **John Attridge** has dedicated his career to helping companies unlock their potential through innovative barter and trade solutions. By guiding businesses to optimise their resources, boost sales, and achieve sustainable growth, his expertise has empowered organisations to leverage their untapped assets. In an increasingly competitive marketplace, John's strategic approach has created new opportunities, enabling companies to thrive and adapt in a rapidly changing economic landscape.

Similarly, **Volker Jaeckel**'s focus on innovation and commitment to excellence have established him as a key figure in marketing and business strategy. Renowned for his sharp business acumen, Volker consults and advises organisations on how to navigate the complexities of modern commerce with strategic vision and precision. Through his expertise, he empowers businesses to adapt and thrive in an ever-changing marketplace.

Another expert on growth is **Ian Fishwick**, a "serial acquirer" in the tech industry who has dedicated his career to driving exponential growth, fostering small businesses, and supporting technological innovation. His focus on expanding broadband access to rural areas reflects his commitment to bridging the digital divide, ensuring underserved communities have the tools they need to thrive in today's interconnected world. Through strategic acquisitions and a visionary approach, Ian has propelled his companies to new heights, contributing significantly to the development of technologies that empower both people and businesses.

As CEO of Unipart, **Darren Leigh** serves as an inspiring example for those seeking to bypass traditional academic routes into the workforce. Starting as an apprentice, Darren's journey to the top showcases the power of hard work, determination, and the valuable opportunities that apprenticeships offer for building a successful and fulfilling career.

Mike Radoor exemplify the power of imagination, creativity, and unconventional approaches to business success. Mike, a serial entrepreneur, author, and keynote speaker, has over a decade of experience in building and scaling multimillion-dollar companies. After facing the challenges of rapid growth and severe burnout, Mike shifted his focus. Now, he uses his extensive experience to help businesses transform by promoting mindset shifts and implementing practical strategies for sustainable success.

Similarly, **Chris Browne**, drawing on his role as Ted Baker's Global Retail Executive, shares valuable insights through his training sessions and keynote speeches. His dynamic leadership and innovative retail strategies inspire professionals in the fashion industry and beyond, emphasising the importance of creativity, customer experience, and brand development. Chris's expertise continues to shape how businesses approach innovation and drive growth in a constantly evolving market.

At the forefront of digital marketing, analytics, and advertising, **Abraham Charles** has made a name for himself by collaborating with several A-list clients. His expertise lies in delivering high-impact, data-driven results that help brands enhance their presence in a crowded marketplace. With innovative strategies and a keen understanding of consumer behaviour, Abraham illustrates how effective digital marketing can transform a business's reach and engagement. His ability to harness data and insights allows brands to connect more meaningfully with their audiences, driving success in today's competitive landscape.

Personal stories often leave the deepest impact, and **Gayatree Dipchan**'s account of her traumatic experiences is one of the most harrowing I've encountered. Her journey through profound adversity—and her unwavering determination to rise above it—is a true testament to human resilience. Now, as a practising psychologist specialising in sexual and violent trauma, Gayatree offers vital support to individuals who have faced similar struggles, transforming her own pain into a source of healing for others. Her story beautifully illustrates how personal suffering can fuel compassion and drive the desire to make a meaningful difference.

Kevin Hines shares a similar path, and speaking with him was one of the most enlightening experiences I've had regarding mental health. I remember a time when mental health issues were heavily stigmatised, but we've made great strides since then—thanks in large part to people like Kevin, who bravely share their personal battles to help others.

Kevin, known for surviving his jump from the Golden Gate Bridge, has since become a powerful advocate against suicide, using his story to inspire, educate, and save countless lives. His raw honesty and unwavering commitment to raising awareness about mental illness have paved the way for conversations that once seemed out of reach. Kevin's journey is a testament to the fact that recovery is not only possible but also that one person's courage to share their experience can create a profound ripple effect, touching and transforming the lives of many.

Bridging the gap between mental health discussions and corporate culture, **Carla Berbary** is making a significant impact through her mental health workshops, where she equips employees with practical tools and strategies to improve their well-being. Her sessions are both engaging and interactive, focusing on stress management, resilience-building, and maintaining a healthy work-life balance. By creating a supportive and open environment for honest conversations, Carla's work fosters a culture that prioritises mental well-being, ultimately leading to healthier, more productive teams.

Nick and Melissa Stehr have defied the conventional statistics surrounding teenage love. After twenty-six years of marriage and a successful business partnership, they have transformed what many consider a challenge into a remarkable success story. Their journey demonstrates that early relationships, often met with skepticism, can evolve into lifelong partnerships when built on mutual respect, dedication, and shared values. Their personal and professional lives stand as proof that young love can lead to enduring fulfillment and achievement, reminding us that every story is unique and that statistics do not define individual destinies.

During my time at Reebok, I learned that innovation is the cornerstone of any successful endeavour. This belief was further reinforced during my conversation with **Dr. Armine Arezki**, who holds a PhD in Robotics. Dr. Arezki masterfully combines his expertise in technology with his passions for art and sports, resulting in products that are both groundbreaking and inspiring. Our discussion was a powerful reminder that the most impactful progress emerges when we courageously unite different disciplines and perspectives.

As we delve into the lives of these remarkable individuals, let their journeys inspire you to harness your own strengths, confront adversity, and strive for greatness. Together, we can continue to lift each other up and create a world where resilience and compassion lead the way. Welcome to *Survive and Thrive II*—a celebration of the human spirit and the power of community to inspire transformation and forge a brighter future.

RICK MACCI
Hall of Fame Tennis Coach

Rick Macci

Beyond its iconic design, Reebok has always been synonymous with sports performance, which made meeting Rick Macci an absolute privilege. We discovered several shared experiences, from appearing on international TV stations and authoring books to mentoring some of the brightest talents. When Rick was coaching Serena and Venus Williams, they were wearing Reebok. However, our commonalities soon diverge when it comes to Rick's extraordinary achievements in the world of tennis. A former player himself, Rick has been named USA National Coach of the Year seven times and has coached five players to the world number one ranking. His relentless dedication and unparalleled expertise have rightfully earned him a place in both the US Professional Tennis Association Florida Hall of Fame and the National Hall of Fame, where he remains the youngest-ever inductee.

Rick Macci's story is truly remarkable, especially considering that he didn't pick up a tennis racket until he was twelve years old. Today, he teaches more lessons than anyone else in the United States, embodying his belief that "if you have passion and work hard, you can achieve anything."

Growing up in Greenville, Ohio, Rick faced challenges early on. His father passed away when he was just ten, leaving Rick, his sister, and their mother to navigate life on their own. At twelve, with nothing but a brick wall to practice against, Rick discovered tennis and "instantly fell in love with the game." His passion and relentless work ethic paid off; by the age of eighteen, he was the number one player in the Ohio Valley. Reflecting on his journey, Rick humbly attributes his rapid rise to "a lot of hard work, dedication, and good athleticism."

"It's not a straight line to the top."

By the age of twenty-two, Rick made the pivotal decision to pursue coaching, explaining, "I enjoyed helping others more than focusing on myself, and that remains the cornerstone of who I am." Now, at the age of sixty-nine, Rick's passion for coaching is as strong as ever, affirming, "I love it just as much now as I did back then."

Rick is the epitome of a 'glass half full' person. He believes, "When you love something and have a constant drive to improve, that positivity becomes the force that helps you overcome any obstacle." This optimistic outlook shapes his own approach and allows him to "sprinkle that positivity down to others," transforming how they perceive challenges and solve problems. In the context of tennis, where setbacks often come in the form of lost points, cultivating a positive mindset from the outset is crucial. Rick emphasises that this approach helps to "expedite the learning curve," setting the foundation for long-term success.

Rick sees himself as more of a life coach than just a tennis coach, with a focus on mindset and attitude. His lessons are filled with wisdom and insights, such as the advice he gave to Serena Williams, "The only time it's over is when you quit." That nugget changed her mindset; as he shares, "She always felt like she never lost. She just ran out of time. That's how she framed it in her mind." It confirms his belief that it's not the

"A winner finds a way; a loser just finds excuses."

challenges you face, but how you respond to them that truly matters—something he attributes to a positive mindset. His daily routine reflects this philosophy, reinforcing his belief that when you establish the right habits and mindset, "you become a machine," mentally equipped to handle whatever comes your way.

Rick's day begins long before most people have even stirred from their sleep. Rising at 1 a.m., he starts his morning with four yogurts and plenty of water. After spending a few quiet moments with his cat, he heads to his office, where he makes it a point to personally respond to every email within twenty-four hours. Following this, he runs half a mile before returning to his office for virtual meetings with clients from the UK, Belarus, Germany, and beyond.

By 5 a.m., Rick is opening up the Rick Macci Tennis Centre, which is set in a large park in Boca Raton, Florida, and so, as a park ranger, he also personally unlocks the gates. By 6 a.m., he's already on the court, ready to teach. Despite approaching seventy, Rick maintains an intense schedule, teaching fifty hours a week, seven days a week. "That's my routine. I don't deviate," he says with unwavering commitment. After a full day on the courts, he wraps up in his office, where his methodical approach to work shines through: "I'm well-structured; I've got it down to a science." Rick's success is evident, and although he oversees a large team, he remains grounded. You'll still find him picking up rubbish and sweeping floors.

On top of an already gruelling schedule, Rick also raised his three daughters after his divorce. He admits, "I'm very competitive and set in my ways, so it's forced me to listen and see things from a different perspective." Balancing his demanding career with fatherhood has tested his limits and broadened his approach to life and coaching. Rick isn't looking for the perfect student; in fact, he prefers the opposite. "I want the kid with a temper, the one who throws the racket, the one with a different attitude because it's a challenge," he says. It's not just the challenge that excites him; his approach is about tapping into his inner resources to "extract greatness" from these students and help them view the world through a different lens. Building confidence and courage in someone before they even realise they have it is his most rewarding goal. As Rick puts it, "It's the best feeling in the world."

When Rick moved to Florida in 1980, he encountered a man who would become his mentor and "biggest influence"—Dr. James Loehr, a renowned performance psychologist and pioneer in maximising human potential. Rick recalls how Dr. Loehr's approach to "slowing things down in your mind, flipping the script, and seeing things from a different perspective" resonated deeply with him. This new way of thinking shaped Rick's coaching philosophy and validated the perspective he had held since he was thirteen years old.

Rick views coaching as "an art" and acknowledges that his approach varies with each individual. "You've got to know when to push buttons, and when to hug them," he says, emphasising the importance of reading each person's unique needs. For Rick, understanding and responding to the emotional "temperature" of each student is key to effective coaching. With a touch of humour, he even quips that he should be in the Hall of Fame "just for putting up with some of the parents."

The Rick Macci Tennis Academy offers year-round tennis programs, in which Rick is personally involved. He says, "It's the best instruction in the world because it's all backed up by science." Not only that, Rick is on the 'shop floor,' seven days a week, and is proud to say he leads by example.

His approach to coaching reflects an in-depth understanding of both the mental and physical aspects of sports. By focusing on building mental strength, he helps athletes push beyond their perceived limits, illustrating that success in sports is not solely dependent on natural talent but also on mindset and technique. His work with top players like Andy Roddick, Serena and Venus Williams, Maria Sharapova, and Jennifer Capriati, as well as his experience with over 300 national champions, underscores his expertise in shaping both elite and emerging talent. Rick's belief in the power of discipline, perspective, and proper mechanics highlights his

commitment to developing well-rounded athletes who can achieve excellence through dedication and mental fortitude.

Rick emphasises the importance of forging one's own path in life, yet he also feels a strong sense of destiny in his mission to "help others." He believes the people you surround yourself with are crucial, noting that they can have a profound influence, so it's vital to "listen to positive people."

When asked about his proudest moments, Rick's response is strikingly humble. Rather than focusing on the success stories of those who reached the pinnacle of their careers or the numerous Grand Slam victories he's been a part of, Rick finds fulfilment in the everyday impact he makes on ordinary people. This perspective highlights his belief that true success isn't just about accolades or high-profile achievements but about the meaningful connections and positive influences we can offer to those around us.
According to Rick, success isn't defined by money: "It's being consistent, delivering the goods on a regular basis, even though there's turbulence."

Coaching in the twenty-first century has enabled Rick to enhance his sessions with technology, "accelerating the learning curve more efficiently." By using his phone on the court, he can slow down performances and show students "exactly what's breaking down biomechanically" or even provide them with examples like "what Roddick did on his serve."

"Greatness is defined by consistency."

While technology has significantly impacted the sport, Rick also acknowledges its downsides, noting that many people seek a "quick fix" and rely on videos that "just regurgitate a lot of technical information" without the real expertise to back it up. For Rick, being coached is not about watching a few videos; it's about "making yourself uncomfortable so you can get more comfortable." As a coach, you push your students to "keep building and building until they have enough glue and substance to take them through the turbulence."

Rick emphasises that as a coach, "You've got to love people and love what you do. You've got to love helping others more than helping yourself, and you need to have an incredible passion because it's a never-ending job." He understands human nature deeply and suggests that "people are lazy, so any coach has to approach their work with that mindset." For Rick, coaching isn't just about teaching tennis; "it's about making a difference in someone's life." At Rick Macci's Tennis Academy, tennis is a sport for everyone, and no one is excluded from reaching their personal best. With the confidence of a world-class coach, he asserts, "If someone's a donkey, I can't make them a thoroughbred, but I can make them the best donkey they can be."

At sixty-nine, Rick boasts boundless energy and aims to maintain his rigorous schedule for another twenty years. He attributes his vitality to a disciplined routine, taking "about twenty vitamins" a day, eating only chicken, and prioritising sleep. "When you get into a routine, you become a machine, and machines are tough to beat," he asserts.

While most people might consider retirement, Rick seems to be just getting started. Balancing the care of his three daughters, managing a large and busy business, coaching duties, and attending to employees, he remains highly active. He attributes his stamina and focus to "mindset, mind control, and perspective." With his direct number listed on his website, it's understandable that he avoids outside distractions to stay committed to what is important to him.

"Don't let the situation control you; you control the situation."

"If you're not getting better, you're getting worse."

HOW TO
SURVIVE
AND
THRIVE
VOLUME II

IAN FISHWICK

Chairman of Airband, Author of *The Street-Smart MBA*,
Cabinet Office SME Panel, M&A Consultant

Ian Fishwick

My perspective on business as being grounded in trust, integrity, and meaningful collaboration resonates with Ian's approach. The emphasis on a handshake being as binding as a contract is a rarity in today's fast-paced, profit-driven world, so it's been refreshing to see that we share similar leadership philosophies, focusing on strong products, filling gaps in the market, and fostering teamwork. And, as I always like to point out, it's crucial to remember that amidst all the hard work, you must have fun—an often overlooked element in building sustainable success.

"There are only three reasons for buying a business: economies of scale, geographical expansion, and acquiring a new product or skillset. Be clear before you buy."

Growing up in Wigan, coincidentally not far from me, Ian was shaped by a traditional working-class household where his father, an electrician, was the sole breadwinner, and his mother, like many women in the area, managed the home and family. Attending the local comprehensive school, Ian was given the chance to study computers—an unusual opportunity at the time, which sparked his interest in technology.

His big break came when he was accepted into an accountancy training programme at Pilkington Glass, one of the region's major employers. It was here that Ian's real education began, as he gained hands-on experience in business operations and financial management. By the age of twenty-one, Ian had qualified as an accountant, and with his dual expertise in computers and finance, he quickly found his skills in high demand.

Ian's career took a significant leap forward when he joined Marconi, a leading defence company, as they were modernising through computerisation. Ian's technical and financial acumen made him indispensable during this time of transformation. This could be seen as luck or what Ian describes as being ready to seize opportunities when they materialise.

After successfully computerising the finance department at Marconi, the company aimed to extend this transformation to its factory operations. Ian was tasked with implementing the first-ever manufacturing resource planning system, a pivotal step in modernising production. Reflecting on his time at Marconi, Ian explains, "This was the place that built all the top-secret encryption equipment, including the phone Margaret Thatcher used to speak with Ronald Reagan." His efforts helped turn a £2.4 million annual loss into a £2 million profit within five years on sales of £22 million.

Ian's career progression was swift, and by thirty, he had become the youngest boss at Marconi. But he didn't just stop there. By thirty-five, Ian was Managing Director of Telewest North West, an internet and cable company operating at a time when the UK was the only country allowing its citizens to buy internet access for their home, cable TV, and telecoms, from the same company, something he describes as "a practically unbelievable situation now, but we were innovating on a massive scale and setting global standards."

He recalls, "We expanded from just four TV channels to over 200, launching, amongst others, Sky Sports and Sky Movies. I ran the first trials of 50 Mbps internet access in 1997. It was a fascinating time."

Ian oversaw operations across most of the North West, stretching from Liverpool to the edge of Manchester and north to Blackpool. When Ian took over in 1996, the company was at rock bottom, consistently ranking near the lowest on almost every key business metric. In hindsight, Ian admits, "It was possibly the biggest gamble of my life."

However, under his leadership, the company became known for breaking what he calls "the unholy triangle," becoming the fastest-growing cable firm in the UK, and winning the prestigious Industry National Customer Service Award, all while maintaining its position as the lowest-cost operator within the group.

"We weren't just launching the world's most innovative technologies; everything about the business had never been done before, so we designed all the support systems as we went along. To take a business from nearly the worst in the UK to the best is up there with one of my proudest moments."

However, in 2000, Ian was made redundant when the business he helped grow consolidated from four separate companies to a single national network. Reflecting on this experience, Ian shares a valuable lesson: "When I sat and thought about it, I realised that redundancy doesn't mean you're a bad person. It's not an appraisal of your worth or performance. I'd had a fabulous and successful career. I was down to a shortlist of two people to run the UK business, but someone must come second. Redundancy is often the result of business reorganisation, and the higher up the organisation you are, the more likely you are to be impacted by it."

Nevertheless, his pragmatic approach turned what could have been a setback into an opportunity. Change came swiftly for Ian when he received a call from a US-based company that had recently acquired seven telecom firms in the UK. They offered him a job, and he rapidly transformed Netnet from seven separate entities into a unified company. More impressively, under his leadership, the business went from a £20 million loss to £1.6 million profit in just 16 months, which Ian still considers "the greatest turnaround" of his career.

Despite this remarkable success, the waters didn't remain calm, and Netnet's US parent company eventually filed for Chapter 11 bankruptcy, leaving Ian to tell his 450 UK employees that they were closing the business because they could not repay their debts. It was a harsh reminder of how external circumstances can override even the most successful efforts. Ian says, "If you work for a subsidiary, it will always be the financial health of the group that will ultimately determine what happens."

Like many of his former employees, Ian unexpectedly found himself in limbo. He went home, waiting for the phone to ring. He struggled to reconcile how, after achieving so much, things could have gone so disastrously wrong and ended up being made redundant twice in 18 months. It was a moment of deep reflection, one that highlighted the unpredictability of even the most successful careers. It took Ian about six or seven months to come to terms with his situation, realising that it was time for him to start his own business. After the dot-com bubble burst, raising funds proved nearly impossible, with banks hesitant to invest. But his luck changed when he reconnected with a former boss who believed in him. In 2003, the two partnered, starting with next to nothing, and together, they built a business that eventually achieved a £70 million turnover and was sold in a £100m transaction. This venture marked a turning point, proving Ian's resilience and entrepreneurial spirit.

As the founder and CEO of AdEPT Technology Group plc, Ian initially attracted several private investors and positioned the company as a "serial acquirer." He outlines his strategic approach, noting, "There are only three reasons for buying any company: economies of scale, geographic expansion, and acquiring new products or skill sets."

Within a remarkably short timeframe, he led the flotation of AdEPT on the London Stock Exchange's AIM in 2006. This achievement underscored Ian's leadership skills and highlighted his ability to navigate the complex landscape of the tech industry, building a company that thrived through strategic acquisitions and innovative growth. Throughout his career, Ian has orchestrated an impressive forty-three mergers and acquisitions in the UK tech industry, honing his expertise in "putting businesses together and making them more profitable."

Reflecting on his business philosophy, Ian states, "People come to me to sell their business because I have a reputation for being honourable. I pay a fair price and never try to get out of paying. I agree before the acquisition what will happen to all the people." This clear, focused approach, paired with a tenacious spirit, has been central to Ian's ability to drive growth and unlock value in every business he touches. He explains, "No matter what was thrown at me, I never, ever went backwards." And, throughout a twenty-nine-year career, Ian reported increased operating profits every year without fail.

He points out that fourteen of the twenty-nine years were spent navigating economic recession or uncertainty, making his achievements even more remarkable: "A CEO should never tell themselves that things will be okay when the economy returns to normal, as history shows that, on average, over the longer term, every other year, there is an economic problem of some sort." His resilience in the face of challenges has been a defining trait, enabling him to thrive in environments where many would falter.

Ian has a keen appreciation for detail and statistics. He points out that while there are 8,000 large businesses in the UK, approximately 2.5 million smaller enterprises employ around 61% of the entire workforce. This statistic highlights his belief that, despite the focus often placed on large corporations, smaller businesses can wield significant influence over the economy.

He challenges us, "Just imagine if those 2.5 million small businesses employed just one more person." Ian argues that the key to economic growth lies in fostering an environment where small businesses can thrive, particularly by making it easier to secure government contracts, especially those valued at less than £5 million. His insights reflect a solid commitment to empowering smaller enterprises as a driving force behind economic progress.

"Track your company's bank balance on a graph every morning. Over time, patterns will emerge, and you will better understand how payroll, supplier payments, and VAT bills affected your cash flow."

As a published author of *The Street-Smart MBA - Mastering Business Acumen Without Going To School,* Ian offers tips and advice about business fundamentals, sharing stories and anecdotes from his three decades as a business leader. "It's teaching people the basics of money management and concentrating on not just the warnings but also some of the tricks," he says.

Ian stresses that many people entering business mistakenly focus solely on profits without understanding the complexities of cash flow. He highlights that the best leaders know exactly how much money they have and what they're due to spend in the coming weeks.

Reflecting on his own experience, he shares how his team would track their bank balance on a graph every morning, and over time, patterns emerged. After three months, they understood how payroll, supplier payments, and VAT bills affected their cash flow. This simple, disciplined approach taught them how their business truly operated.

"A business will never work unless there is a clear demand for what you're trying to sell."

Ian still prefers doing business the old-fashioned way, stating, "If I shake your hand, then I expect you to honour the deal." As a manager, he upholds the principle of "treating others how you'd like to be treated." Reflecting on leadership, Ian is deeply concerned about the behaviour of some modern leaders, particularly those in business and politics. He believes they set a poor example for young people when they act as though laws don't matter and lying is acceptable. "That's not how I grew up, and I don't see it as a step forward. I'd like to turn it back," he says.

He worries about leaders who fail to grasp the impact of being a role model, expressing concern about the growing influence of some billionaires who disregard employment laws and ethical responsibilities. Ian warns of the dangers of creating a society where wealth and power allow leaders to bypass accountability and forsake a longer-term outlook on the health of societies and the planet. Integrity is being lost in the pursuit of short-term inflated valuations and ego, a trend he finds troubling for the future.

With his clear focus and practical approach, Ian's leadership extends beyond his own businesses. He is part of the UK Cabinet Office's Small to Medium Enterprise Panel, where he advises the government on ways to place more contracts with small companies. As Chairman of Airband, in some ways, he returns to his roots, building an independent internet service provider. Ian remains deeply involved in technological innovations, helping bring superfast broadband to rural and hard-to-reach areas. This role reflects his commitment to supporting both emerging businesses and cutting-edge industries.

Ian's journey from a boy in Wigan who didn't make it into grammar school to a successful entrepreneur who founded a business from his spare room and later sold it for £100 million is remarkable. Along the way, he completed forty-three technology mergers and acquisitions and even authored his own book—and he isn't stopping there. He is now taking his experience of buying and merging companies into corporate finance to help the next generation of 'serial acquirers.' His story is one of resilience, vision, and determination.

"Consistency as a business is key. My mentor described it as like a potter's wheel—as soon as you take your eye off the ball, it's just a pile of clay again."

HOW TO
SURVIVE
AND
THRIVE
VOLUME II

MIRELA SULA

CEO and Founder of *Global Woman Magazine* and *Global Woman Club*

Mirela Sula

What I found most compelling about Mirela is her attitude toward life and her extraordinary ability to reinvent herself in order to thrive. Having grown up in a small and limiting environment, Mirela possessed a unique determination; she refused to accept the future laid out for her and instead chose to carve her own path. Not only did she succeed in doing so, but she also found the strength, energy, and conviction to help other women do the same, never content to simply rest on her achievements.

Born and raised in Albania, Mirela had a happy childhood until her parents' divorce changed everything. At that time, divorce was still considered socially unacceptable under the communist regime. Mirela's life changed dramatically when her mother, a midwife and political activist with considerable influence, went into self-imposed exile and moved to the mountains.

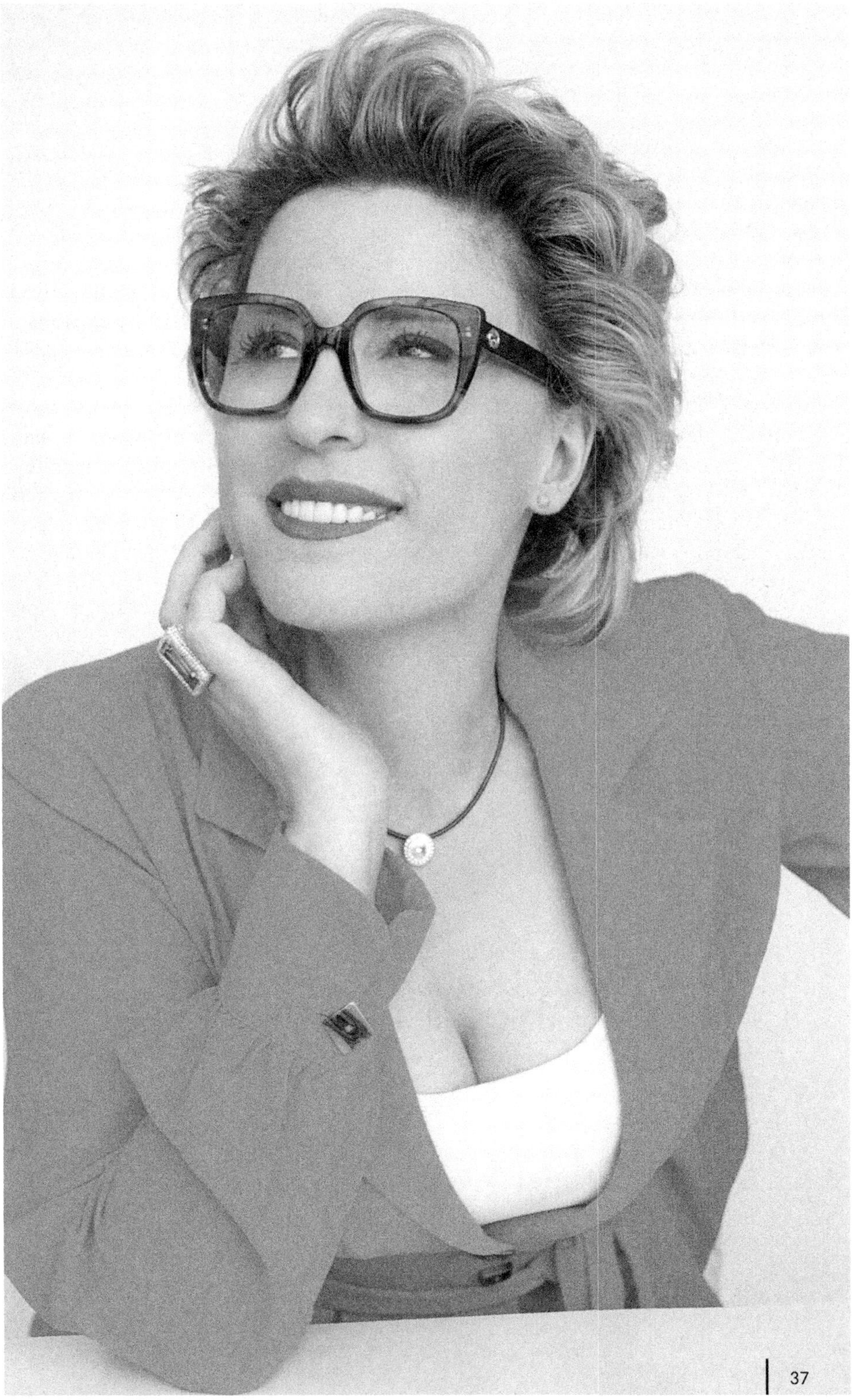

It felt like a form of punishment for Mirela, as if her mother had transgressed some unspoken rule, and a profoundly dark period ensued as she witnessed the constant abuse and mistreatment of her brother and mother at the hands of her stepfather.

Despite being an A* student who loved studying, she was often called "stupid" by her family, and so reading became her escape from a difficult home life. She explains, "I often used my imagination to transport myself to another world, and that saved me."

Reflecting on this "very dark moment," Mirela recalls feeling deeply isolated, which she believes played a pivotal role in her decision to marry at just eighteen. "It was a form of escapism," she explains. "I didn't want to return home after finishing college, so I saw marriage as the beginning of my adult life." She moved in with her husband's large family in a remote village, where her days were consumed with tasks like milking cows, cleaning, washing, and serving the eight men in the family. However, she was also given the opportunity to attend university. It was part of an agreement she made with her husband: if he wanted to marry her, he had to allow her to pursue higher education, and he agreed.

"If you give up and do not believe, nothing will come to you."

While at university, she was offered a job as a teacher in the village. She taught twenty children and loved it so much that she spent two years persuading her husband to move to the village and become part of the community.

Just as things were starting to look up for Mirela, her life was turned upside down when she became pregnant and gave birth to her child, who tragically passed away at just six months old. She tumbled into a deep depression, intensified by the lack of understanding and support around her. This heartbreaking experience, and becoming pregnant again with her second child, marked the beginning of a new journey for Mirela—one of healing and self-discovery. She realised she had to either "find a path to light or give up entirely."

Mirela moved to Tirana, Albania's capital, to ensure her son had access to medical care, and a whole new world opened up to her. Coming from a small mountaintop village, moving to a vibrant big city "allowed her to see the world differently," and she decided to separate from her husband.

As a newly single mother, Mirela's life had opened up, and her path to healing led to a desire to heal others, so she decided to pursue studies in psychology, positive psychotherapy, and family therapy. Looking back on her journey, Mirela believes that new opportunities can arise from trauma, pain, and adversity when you are able to

"A problem is a problem when we allow it to be bigger than us."

"forgive those who shaped the painful path that led you to become who you are today."

After several years of writing for publications and lecturing in psychology, she created the *Psychologist Magazine* and began to focus on the empowerment of women. She still remembers what life was like for her mother and grandmother in Albania and has vivid memories of her own experiences, including having to ask permission to leave the house.

It wasn't long before Mirela felt the need to "move on, develop [herself], and grow" even more, so she decided to study at the University of Sheffield, where she obtained a Master's in Counselling and Psychology. She later obtained a further Master's in Positive Psychotherapy and began running workshops to support women affected by domestic violence.

> **"You can't use your power unless you first see it, realise it, and accept it. Then, you can claim it."**

While on a trip to London, she then impulsively decided to quit her various jobs, get a student visa, and return to take a PhD in Psychology. She feels that coming to London was part of her destiny, and it helped her realise that she has power over her own life. She reveals, "When I started empowering myself, I didn't see my husband at the time as a powerful man anymore. I saw him as somebody who was suppressing my feminine power."

She taught at three different universities and founded and was Editor-in-Chief of *Global Woman Magazine*, a publication platform dedicated to empowering women in business. Mirela then went on to found Global Woman Club, which now has clubs in twenty-seven countries and helps thousands of women unlock their potential personally and professionally. She has also published over ten books and has appeared on television as a psychologist, offering tips and advice on love.

In just a decade, Mirela was able to completely transform her life, proving how much you can achieve with the right mindset. She claims, "When people get stuck in powerlessness, fear, and pain, all they need to understand is that power is not physical, it's mental. And if they learn how to strengthen their minds, how to use their thoughts, and how to turn their mental capacities into their advantage, they can overcome any situation."

In empowering herself, Mirela realised she could take control of her life on her own terms, making her own decisions about who she wanted in her life, where she wanted to go, and how she wanted to live. She emphasises the importance of women reclaiming their power for the betterment of the world, explaining that it all "starts from the family." For Mirela, "If the family is in harmony, it creates a strong, positive presence in the quantum space. When every woman harmonises with herself, her partner, and her children, it creates a ripple effect." She believes that women must reclaim their power, not out of ego, but out of a responsibility to bring positive change to the world.

As the Founder and CEO of Global Woman Club, she focuses on empowering women to fulfil their dreams. She encourages women to tap into their "feminine energy and intuition," teaching them how to develop these qualities by ascending a pyramid that represents survival, success, and, ultimately, significance. While men often seek success,

"We should be grateful to have so many opportunities, but we also need to tap into these opportunities and empower ourselves."

she argues, women desire significance; they aim to reach the very top of the pyramid.

Having come from a place where she "lacked the power and support" she needed, Mirela developed a deep desire to help others facing similar struggles. Her mission has been to support women in transforming "from powerless to empowered, from hurt to impactful, using their pain to heal others."

She suggests that several factors can influence our journeys, such as the "genes of our parents and ancestors, which play a role in shaping who we become." She also identifies environmental factors as a "massive force driving us toward our destination," claiming that it can even alter the cells in our body. She believes this is one of the reasons she is now a completely different person from the powerless young woman she once was, with no voice or direction, living in the mountains of Albania. She declares, "I've told the world that I've killed my old self; she's no longer alive. There's no trace of her, no cells, no stories, nothing. It's a new woman with a new mission."

The new Mirela sees integrity as one of the most important qualities you can have. Using an example, she recalls how, back in January 2018, she was preparing for the Global Woman's Summit when a friend suggested the summit could be held in New York. Mirela agreed and immediately started informing people, who then booked flights for the event to be held in June. Attendees were coming from Germany, Paris, Amsterdam, and Dubai, yet no venue had been booked in New York. While her friend wanted to cancel, having found it difficult to secure a venue, Mirela, with her strong sense of integrity, refused and continued to organise the event on her own. Flying out to New York for the first time, with only one month before the summit, she managed to secure the perfect place, the Sheraton Hotel in Manhattan, with 300 people flying in to attend.

She knew early on that she wanted "to stand for something big," but she also knew that she "had to start small." For Mirela, this meant borrowing money and organising the Migrant Woman Conference. As an immigrant herself, she had a strong sense of the support needed for other women in her position in order to tackle issues, such as language barriers, when integrating into a new and unfamiliar country. The event, held at the Hilton in London's Covent Garden, was a big success and put her on the map. She was invited to talk on BBC Radio 4's Women's Hour, and doors started to open, including an invitation to speak at a "massive investment forum in China." She later opened up her office in Liverpool Street, and her enterprise grew, franchising it to twenty-seven countries around the globe.

The little girl from a remote village in Eastern Europe grew up to travel the world and earn an income most people only dream of. She bought her own home, and during the COVID-19 pandemic, while much of the world was shut down, Mirela was busy "building an empire." Today, her app boasts over 30,000 members, complete with a members' portal, an online academy, and a virtual business school. She's also created an online events platform with easy-to-use templates designed for 'tech-phobic' members.

But Mirela hasn't stopped there. She founded the Global Men's Club and the Investors Club and currently manages five magazines. To top it all off, she also found love and a collaborator in life and business. Describing him as her "rock," she is thrilled that he has given up his day job to help her run her growing enterprise.

Rising from the depths of sorrow, Mirela discovered the strength to persevere and thrive in her mission to help others. By surrounding herself with supportive people who align with her values, Mirela embodies the belief that any challenge can be conquered with the right mindset.

"The definition of success is you start and you complete. The definition of failure is that you quit."

HOW TO
SURVIVE
AND
THRIVE
VOLUME II

DARREN LEIGH

CEO of Unipart

Darren Leigh

D arren and I both come from modest backgrounds, yet we've each shown a strong entrepreneurial spirit grounded in the belief that personal responsibility is crucial in shaping one's own destiny. While Darren has dedicated his career to optimising supply chains, making them more efficient, resilient, and sustainable, my focus has been driving innovation to establish Reebok as a global brand. On the surface, we might not seem to have much in common, but when you dig deeper, you'll see the common threads that bind us—a shared commitment to growth, adaptability, and a long-term vision for success.

Darren was born in 1972 to a "working-class" family in Ilkeston, Derbyshire, in the Midlands. Once a mining town in the 1960s, the area had since shifted to textile manufacturing. Darren's parents separated when he was still young, leaving his mother, Jeanette, to work long hours to provide for Darren and his sister, and his maternal grandparents to play a significant role in his upbringing. His grandfather, in particular, became a key figure during these formative years. "He was a very positive influence," Darren recalls. His grandfather's steady guidance imparted values of perseverance, humility, and a deep sense of responsibility that would shape Darren's future outlook on life and work.

Darren remembers his school days fondly, though he admits, "I didn't do phenomenally well academically, but I enjoyed the social side." Beyond the friendships and camaraderie, school felt more like a place of conformity than exploration: "It wasn't a place that encouraged you to think for yourself or challenge things. Instead, it was more about doing your work and staying quiet." This lack of stimulation left Darren restless, and by the time he was sixteen, he decided to leave school early and enter the workforce.

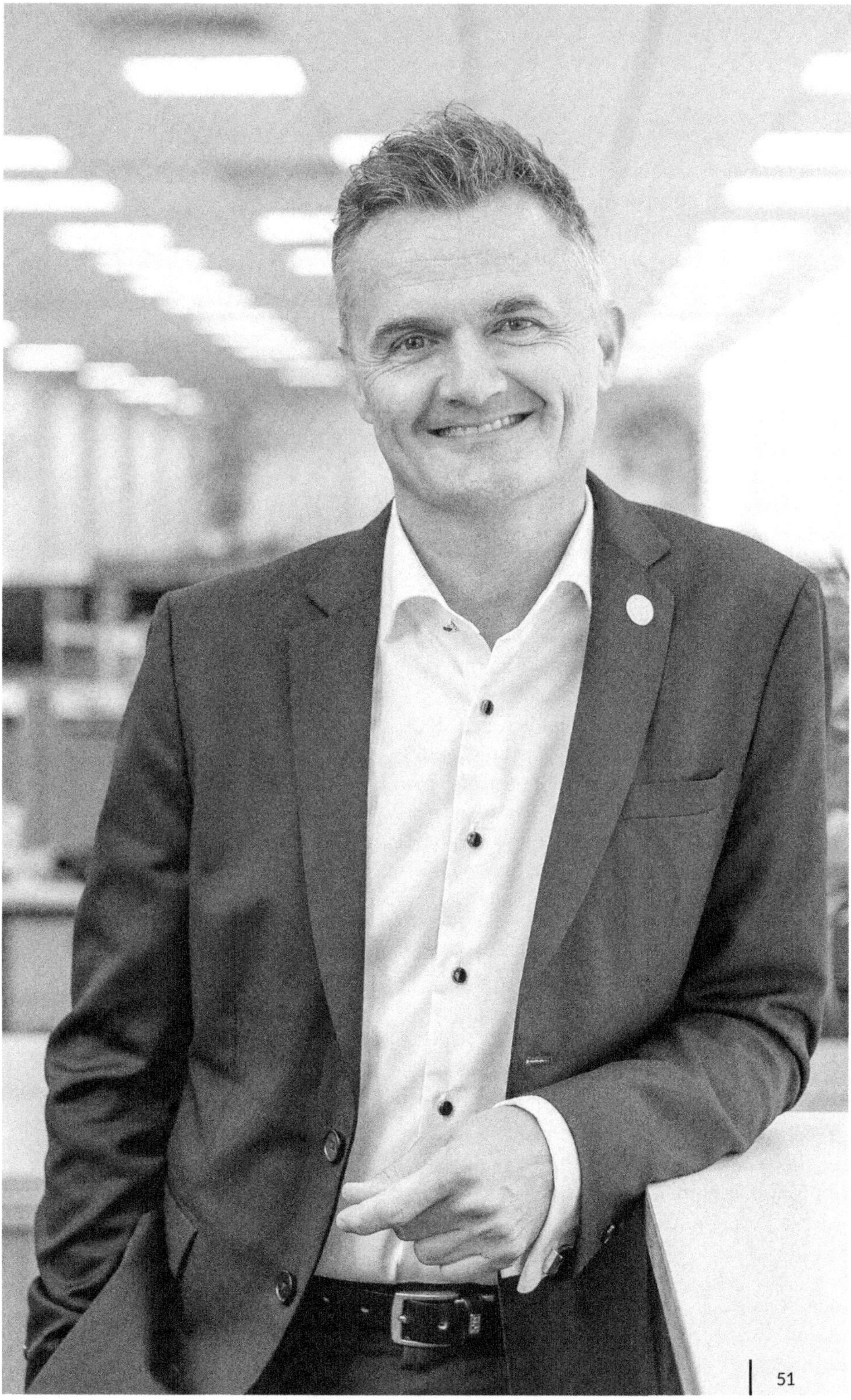

This first step into the professional world came through an apprenticeship at a local manufacturing company. For Darren, this was more than just a job. It offered him a broad range of experiences, rotating him through various departments and giving him insight into how each part of the company functioned. From sales to finance, Darren not only learned the mechanics of the business but also the importance of relationships, communication, and problem-solving.

Starting in the sales department, his tasks were modest—filing paperwork, answering phones, and "making endless cups of tea." But Darren knew this was part of the learning process, and after a few months, he moved into the Sales Ledger Department, where he began developing his financial acumen. By the time he was seventeen, Darren's hard work paid off when he was promoted to Purchase Ledger Supervisor. This was no small feat for someone so young, and it represented the first real validation of his abilities and impact in the workplace.

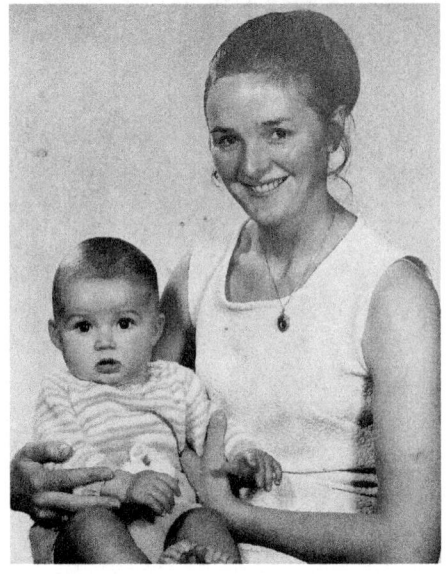

Although Darren may have bypassed a traditional university education, he remained committed to his studies, and by twenty-two, he was in the final year of his professional accountancy qualification. He then took a position with Northern Foods, a significant manufacturer employing tens of thousands of people. While he initially viewed it as a prestigious career move with higher pay, it quickly became a lesson in the importance of asking the right questions before committing to a role. He reflects, "During the interview process, I was so focused on the allure of a big name and a pay rise that I overlooked other critical factors."

This experience taught Darren that success wasn't just about climbing the corporate ladder but about making informed decisions and ensuring the right fit between personal values and professional goals. When the next opportunity came along at Coats PLC, Darren was prepared. He joined the company at just twenty-three as the Finance Manager, tasked with establishing new accounting processes and implementing cost and productivity reporting frameworks to improve the business's performance. This time, he asked the right questions, ensuring that the role was aligned with his career aspirations and would offer room for growth.

As Darren's career progressed, so did the complexity of his responsibilities. Moving into senior leadership positions brought new challenges, mainly regarding managing teams and navigating difficult situations. One of the critical lessons Darren learned early on was the importance of staying calm under pressure.

"The first thing to do in a crisis is demonstrate leadership and take control. You've got to avoid panic and avoid letting the rest of the organisation feel like things are spiralling out of control," Darren explains. In times of crisis, whether it's a financial downturn or a logistical challenge, Darren believes in leading with transparency. "You can't hide problems from your team. You must be upfront about what's happening, the potential impact, and what needs to be done."

For Darren, this approach has been crucial in maintaining the confidence and morale of his teams. His ability to manage crises effectively is a skill that Darren attributes not only to his personal experience but also to the mentors who have shaped his leadership style.

Darren has been in his most recent role for two years, serving as the CEO of Unipart, a UK-based global supply chain leader, offering everything from manufacturing to logistics to technology solutions, serving various sectors including healthcare, technology, e-commerce, consumer and retail, aerospace, defence, and industrial. After serving as Unipart's Chief Financial Officer, he was promoted to CEO, stepping into the shoes of John Neil, who had led the company for over forty years. This transition was a significant moment, not just for Darren but for Unipart as a whole. "I had the opportunity of working side by side with John for two and a half years," Darren says. The close partnership between the two leaders made the handover smoother than it might have otherwise been, especially during a period marked by global challenges such as the COVID-19 pandemic, the Suez Canal blockage, and the war in Ukraine.

Mentorship has played a vital role throughout Darren's career, and he is quick to acknowledge the influence of those who have helped him along the way. "I've been fortunate to have some very generous people share their time and ideas with me," he says. Three key figures stand out in Darren's memory: Derek Henshaw, who was a generous and unassuming individual who took Darren under his wing when he was just seventeen; Massimo Petronio, a supply chain professional and figure of authority at Coats PLC for over thirty-five years; and Steve Hare, the CEO of Sage PLC, whose leadership has had a lasting impact on Darren's own approach to business. Whether through formal mentorship programmes or informal advice, Darren is committed to helping others navigate their careers with the same support and encouragement he received.

One of the ways Darren has institutionalised this commitment is through Unipart's early careers programme, which brings in a new intake of graduates each year to gain hands-on experience across the business. "It's a very practical-based curriculum, complemented by classroom-based learning," Darren explains. This initiative reflects his belief in the value of diverse experiences and real-world learning, principles that have been central to his own success.

Leading the Unipart Group, Darren elaborates on the company's diverse and integrated approach to supply chain solutions and performance improvement technologies. "We have capabilities that span the entire supply chain," he explains, "from consultancy around supply chain and business transformation to providing logistics services, warehousing, and transportation, and even extending to product design, engineering, and manufacturing."

"Make sure people are aware of the work you're doing."

Unipart's strength lies in its diverse and comprehensive approach. Darren points out the scale of their operations: "If you look at our business, we have 12,500 colleagues operating out of eighty-five locations around the world—forty-five of those are in the UK. And then we have forty locations in twenty countries where we support our customers' global supply chains." This global reach, combined with strong UK-based manufacturing, positions Unipart as a key player in offering tailored solutions across multiple sectors, ensuring businesses operate with greater efficiency, resilience, and sustainability.

As he continues to lead Unipart into the future, Darren remains committed to building a more resilient and self-reliant UK. "We have to play nicely with the rest of the world," he says, "but at the same time, we need to be a little bit more self-sufficient than we are today." Darren explains how Unipart is committed to helping its customers create "more efficient, more resilient, and more sustainable supply chains." In some cases, this means shifting production closer to home. "We have to create here, and we have to own here, rather than being reliant on energy, resources, and products coming from overseas," he asserts.

Darren believes that for the UK to truly prosper, it must prioritise productivity and efficiency, particularly within manufacturing. "We can rebuild a strong manufacturing sector in this country," he insists, "but that requires significant investment, deliberate strategies, and leadership from both the government and from business." He stresses that without active governmental support and policy, this transformation won't take place.

Moreover, Darren emphasises the need to adopt a long-term perspective, urging decision-makers to think beyond immediate gains and consider the impact on future generations. "A crucial part of this," Darren explains, "is developing a genuine concern for those who come after us. The actions we take today must lay the foundation for a more sustainable and self-reliant future." With this in mind, he has shifted his focus toward creating solutions that will benefit generations to come.

"The first thing to do in a crisis is demonstrate leadership and take control."

Looking ahead, Darren sees a significant opportunity in the transition to electric vehicles, noting that this shift has "opened up a new market for unicorn businesses." In response, Unipart is investing in several key areas, including the production of electric batteries for Lotus cars, which is contributing to the push for cleaner transport. In line with this, the company is also committing resources to a "circular economy" with investments such as repurposing and recycling batteries to reduce waste and increase sustainability. Darren envisions a future with more autonomous vehicles, predicting that driverless cars will become the norm, recharging themselves at dedicated points as they integrate seamlessly into modern infrastructure.

Darren's vision for the future is rooted in the lessons of his past. His journey from a sixteen-year-old apprentice to the CEO of a global company is a testament to the power of perseverance, adaptability, and lifelong learning. He believes that for individuals and organisations alike, the key to thriving in an uncertain world is to stay curious, embrace change, work hard, and always keep moving forward. "You are responsible for your own future, and you have to take steps to move in the direction you want to go. At the same time, make sure people are aware of the work you are doing."

"The key to thriving in an uncertain world is to stay curious, embrace change, work hard, and always keep moving forward."

HOW TO
SURVIVE
AND
THRIVE
VOLUME II

Let's share wisdom!

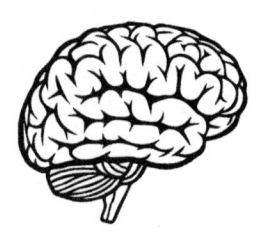

"To live a purposeful life, you must always be learning, growing, and fully expressing yourself."

Adrian Starks
Podcaster, Speaker and Voice Narrator

"The most important thing in life is connecting the mind, body, and spirit. When this happens, you will truly understand who you are."

Alex Da Silva
Co-Founder and COO of Silva Wellness

"When you face challenges, reinvent yourself and return to learning mode."

Amita Vikram Pratap
Brand Strategist

"Don't take yourself too seriously.
Enjoy life."

Alicia Castillo Holley
Founder of Wealthing VC Fund

"Wherever you are right now is exactly where you need to be to learn what you need to create the life or business you want."

Aman Birdi
CEO of Digiruu

"When things seem terrible,
lean hard into gratitude."

Annie Leib
Executive Coach

"We have this inclination to stop and take a break, yet the hack is not to give it all up but rather to hold on to things, even if you're doing it at 10%, keep moving."

Andrew Elliot Stern
Executive Coach

Once you let go of a linear approach and open up to a world made of vibration, you will start becoming more yourself and your vision, accelerating your success."

Arnaud Saint-Paul
Executive Coach

"Every day, send an email to someone who you've never emailed before. The worst thing that can happen is they don't reply. I've had projects, businesses, and job opportunities come from just one email."

Aron Phillips
CEO of RTG Features

"Choose today to be a more positive force for good energy in the world."

April Sabral
CEO of April Sabral Leadership

"Be clear on your strategy. Do you have the right business model? Do you have the right foundations in your business? Once you are there, then you need to understand how to plan successfully, working backward from there."

Athin Cassiotis
Business Growth Expert

"You've got to create a breadcrumb trail for your business. Shift your marketing accordingly."

Barnaby Wynter
Brand Practitioner

"Remember you're where you're supposed to be when you're supposed to be there. Because while change is scary, it also has the power to change your life."

Beth Booker
CEO of Gracie PR

"Only cowards criticise the greatness of people who stand in their power and convictions."

Bonnie Kowaliuk
Mindfulness Coach

"Intentionality gives way to peace and purpose. Adopt a practice of self-awareness so that you can start directing your steps. You have that power to live the life you believe you deserve."

Bridget Hom
Business Life Coach

"Life is not a rehearsal. You are in charge of how this goes, nobody else. When you take back control and release fear - Watch out, here you come."

Bonnie Low-Kramen
Speaker, Author, and Trainer

"Keep going and never quit. This will not only result in success but also fulfilment."

Casey Adams
Founder of listener.com

"Understanding does not require agreement. Different life journeys lead us to different conclusions. But when we respect that, we can love despite the differences and develop new ways to move forward."

Brenda Cox Harkins
Founder of Loud Is Not A Language

"I can't imagine a time in my life when I've gone out to a riverbank or a stream and didn't come out better afterwards. We all need to get outside more to really observe what's going on."

Carla Morris
Executive Director of Sustainably Empowering People Globally

"Embrace the darkness of the journey."

Chris Chambers
Founder, The Turing Forge and Chambers Capital Ventures, Inc.

"Fear of what other people will think is the single most paralysing dynamic in business and in life. You will never own the future if you care what other people think."

Cindy Gallop
Founder and CEO of MakeLoveNotPorn

"On stage, your only job is to make everyone else look good. What if each of us went through life thinking about others and knowing others were thinking about us?"

Chip Brewer
Founder of Growth Story LLC

"By not letting perfect be the enemy of good, we get to keep moving forward."

Chris Kaufman
Co-founder of ArtClvb and StockX

"Develop yourself as a person. Be the best version of you that you can be because this is who you take into your families, your friend groups, your offices, and your business."

Connie Causey Rose
Professional Career Services at Empirejobs

"If you don't ask, you don't get."

Constantine Theodossiou
Money Manager

"Embrace a mindset of continuous learning and an adaptive attitude."

Dr. Anas Bataw
ConTech leader

"Stick to the plan. But allow yourself to be flexible. Embrace change when necessary, especially in response to industry trends, but avoid abandoning your roadmap for every new idea."

Courtney Siegel
VP of Marketing at Skeepers

"When you're facing a problem and unsure how to solve it, change one word in your language. Instead of asking yourself, 'What should I do?' Reframe it and ask yourself, 'What could I do?'"

Daniel Pink
Author

"Be the person you wish was there for you."

David Blake
Motivational Speaker, Facilitator, and Coach

"Persevere and persist against all odds. No matter what your goals are in your life or career, you will come across obstacles. Those should not stop or derail you but instead help you press on."

Dr. Lori A. Manns
CCO at Quality Media Consultant Group LLC

HACIA ATHERTON, CPA, MAPP

International Speaker, Author, 2024 Telstra Best of Business Awards Winner (Vic), Top 100 Women in Construction 2023, 2024 Australian Enterprise Awards: Leading Innovator in Workforce Diversity, Positive Psychology

Hacia Atherton

It's remarkable how we can always find common ground, something that unites us. This was especially evident when I met Hacia Atherton. Although Hacia was born and bred in Australia, both our families originated in Bolton, England, so I was particularly interested in her great-grandfather's story. He ventured to Melbourne and established a plumbing business that still thrives today. This was around the same time my grandfather founded his own running shoe business, JW Foster and Sons. The parallels in our family histories made our connection even more meaningful.

Hacia's first survival moment came when her parents divorced, and at a young age, she moved to the country to live with her mother. Although it was an upheaval leaving the family home and being separated from her father, Hacia found there were positive sides, "with [her] pony, picnics, and exploring the countryside." She also got to return to the city to spend time with her father, who owned a property on the beach, which allowed her to experience the best of all three worlds; the country, city life, and the coast.

No divorce is ideal, but in Hacia's case, it gave her a "very dynamic childhood," and both parents could dedicate a lot of their time to their young daughter. During weekends spent with her sporting father, Hacia developed the resilience and wisdom necessary to thrive in life. She says, "I'd fall off my bike, and [dad] would ask me, 'What would Muhammad Ali say? It's OK to fall, but it's not OK to stay down.'" Her father would set up fake debates around a news topic, get her to read the *Financial Times*, and take her to board meetings. In contrast, her mother gave her a more "feminine" and artistic outlet. Their days were spent collaborating on creative projects, reading Peter Rabbit, and enjoying time in the park.

"In every challenge, there's an opportunity for transformation."

She appeared to have a carefree childhood in a co-ed country school, playing basketball, having mud fights, and climbing trees. But, when she moved back in with her father, she found herself in a private girls' school in Melbourne. It was a big transition that led Hacia to rebel, challenge the teachers, and "end up in the principal's office quite a lot." As an academically strong student, Hacia had many choices but struggled to find her niche. She modelled for a bit before going to university to study law. She then decided the male-dominated legal industry wasn't for her, so she got a qualification in fashion before changing her mind again and starting her own bookkeeping business. After a couple of years of bookkeeping for people in the creative industry, she then did a course in financial planning. Although she enjoyed the job, she explains, "I ran into some conflicts between my value system and how the industry was set up."

Although Hacia knew she didn't want to work in an industry she regarded as "basically a sales machine for financial products and not doing the right thing for many people," she "loved the numbers and working with clients." So, on that basis, Hacia returned to university to study for her bachelor's degree in commerce, majoring in accounting. She was also focused on her talent for dressage, but while training to qualify for the World Equestrian Games in 2017, a few months before her thirtieth birthday, she experienced a horrific horse-riding accident. After falling to the ground, with her 600 kg horse on top of her, she was airlifted to the Alfred Hospital in Melbourne, where she underwent a nine-hour emergency surgery and was told that she may never walk again.

"When women thrive, so does the economy."

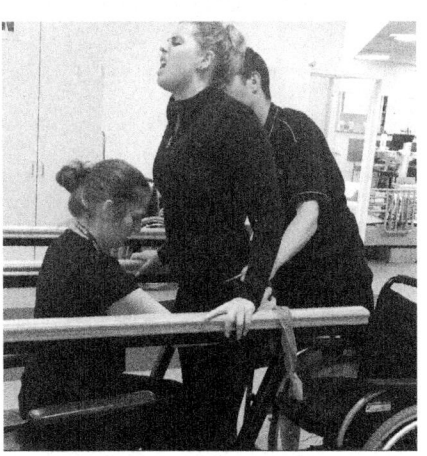

Her pelvis was shattered, both hips were very badly broken, the coccyx and base of her spine were severely damaged, and she suffered significant nerve damage to her right leg. Her father was told that she was only millimetres from death. After three months "pretty much trapped in a hospital bed," she spent another three months learning to stand again. She explains, "I will never be able to describe the pain of being crushed by a horse and the mental struggles of going from a high-level athlete to literally being lifeless in a hospital bed."

It was a moment of pure survival, where Hacia was left entirely reliant on others for things most of us take for granted. The experience of feeling so vulnerable and going from being a very active individual to someone who needed constant care affected her psychologically. She explains, "I became very depressed in the hospital. I was questioning my purpose and the point of life now that I couldn't ride my horses. My whole mind, soul, purpose, identity—everything was gone."

It became clear that it wasn't just her broken body that needed rebuilding; it was her mindset too. Working with her psychiatrists and psychologists, Hacia's perspective began to change, and she started seeing the value of having a "high-quality connection with human beings." She quickly noticed how her life was beginning to improve and how she had discovered a new purpose: "to be the sunshine for other people."

It's a powerful testament to the enduring strength and perseverance of the human spirit that only seven years after the accident, she learned how to walk again and completed a half-marathon and numerous 100k bike rides. She also became a respected speaker on empowerment and psychological well-being. Hacia managed to turn her survival moment into a life where she not only thrives herself but also helps others to do the same.

During Hacia's hospital rehabilitation, she relied on Selgiman's PERMA framework to reframe her mindset, a tool she still uses in her personal and professional life to this day. As a psychological model that builds well-being by focusing on characteristics of positive emotions, relationships, meaning, and accomplishments, Hacia describes how she "would talk to the person next to [her] and tell them about how grateful [they] were to be experiencing this, how advanced the medical technology was, and if [they] had had [those] injuries ten years ago, [they] wouldn't [have been] receiving [that] level of care." Hacia's physiotherapist even commented on how much of a difference her positive attitude and gratitude were having on other patients, noting a marked increase in progress rates between people having rehab sessions with Hacia and those who were not.

117 days after the accident, Hacia was finally able to stand up for a couple of seconds. She was still in a lot of pain and feeling dizzy and nauseous, she slumped back into her wheelchair, feeling utterly defeated. It wasn't until her physiotherapist explained how much those few seconds actually meant that Hacia started to look at things differently. She explains, "Ever since then, in all my work, I make sure people focus on the smallest achievements and take time to celebrate the small steps."

As CEO and Founder of Empowered Women in Trades (EWIT), a social enterprise and charity focused on encouraging women into the skilled trades sector, Hacia speaks about her passion for "supporting vulnerable and at-risk women into meaningful employment and helping them to stay in the industry."

She uses what she has learned from her professional and personal survival experiences to help women working in male-dominated industries. During her work experience in the barrister chambers, she vividly remembers being put off continuing in the profession having witnessed "the horrific treatment of female barristers in the chambers." But she also reflects on the women who stayed in the job, describing them as "trailblazers and strong, courageous fighters."

There are still women like this worldwide, struggling to find their place in a male-dominated skilled trade, and as Hacia

"Feminine energy will often soften the rough side of masculine energy."

explains, "It's a very tough environment." She advises them to celebrate the small achievements, "the fact that you showed up, you stayed on site all day, you came home, and you'll show up again tomorrow."

She uses the social enterprise part of EWIT to work with men, women, and organisations, with all profits going to "benefit vulnerable and at-risk women." The endeavour was set up in some part as a response to the "massive skills shortage" and increasing unemployment rates after the COVID-19 pandemic. Hacia's intention was to "bring these two economic issues together, allowing women to access strong financial careers and resolving the skill shortage."

She's experienced struggles with bureaucracy and aggressive resistance, Even though she admits "there are different challenges" four years on, Hacia is still determined to be the person who "is going to stand up for these women so that they don't run away from what can be a very rewarding career," the same way that she did from a career in law.

It's not just about women; as Hacia suggests, "Bullying and harassment in the skilled trades industry in Australia is a huge problem." She claims the culture in these industries incites male suicide and results in women leaving. Hacia advises that there are simple things you can do to protect yourself from workplace bullying and harassment. Firstly, check whether speaking out is safe; if it's not, then you need to find support outside the workplace. This could be unions, safety officers, or other organisations.

"Success is not a lone-wolf journey; it comes from the collective power of support."

Don't internalise the experience or blame yourself. Ensure you connect with a support network, whether friends, family, a mentor, or a coach. Find someone who can advocate for you if you feel unable to do it yourself.

From a psychological perspective, Hacia can quickly identify the source of bullying and harassment in male-dominated environments, suggesting it will "often happen because the alpha male or the men who are perpetuating this bullying and harassment feel this need to overemphasise their external success and to dominate." Interestingly, she continues to explain how some men may "go into this hypermasculine, aggressive mode… to hunt [women] out of [what could be] a dangerous environment." So, what could be superficially regarded as bullying is perhaps a subconscious attempt to protect. Hacia discusses how, as humans, we all share basic psychological and physical needs such as a "sense of belonging, autonomy, competence, food, water, and shelter." Once these fundamental needs are met, "We begin to see the emergence of different psychological traits between men and women. Women often focus on traits like intuition, nurturing, passion, empathy, and emotional expression, internalising their wounds and struggles. Conversely, men typically exhibit traits such as logic, strength, action, and protection, externalising their wounds and struggles. This externalisation can often be perceived as aggressive and controlling behaviour."

Interestingly, Hacia highlights the difference between how men and women bully. In general, she suggests that men have "a killer shark mindset; they're assertive, logical, strong, and proactive," which can lead to direct bullying, whereas women "tend to do it behind people's backs and try to socially isolate them. They will organise drinks and not invite a certain person, then post those photos on social media." She is clear that it's not related to gender but has more to do with having a masculine or feminine mindset. She suggests that, as humans have progressed, we have become more fluid, with less of a divide between the biological genders. With social media being the main instigator of this change, she states that there is now a general feeling of confusion, resulting in many people feeling lost in their understanding of "what being a human is and what our roles are now in society." To use an example, the fight for women to gain more respect is undermined by an abundance of over-sexualised images on social media. Similarly, she states, "There are also men chopping up wood, with big muscles and tattoos, vying with stay-at-home, nurturing dads." She notes that we, as humans, hold both a psychological masculine and feminine side within us, often sitting predominantly in one but capable of moving between the two ways of thinking and feeling as needed. To combat this, Hacia promotes the importance of "education to teach people how to navigate from their feminine to their masculine side, to identify where they naturally sit."

It may have taken Hacia a while to work out her role in society, but once she found it, her passion for helping empower individuals and spark transformative change has been unwavering. Being able to transform trauma into triumph has made her the perfect advocate for women working in skilled trades and male-dominated industries. As a speaker, consultant, and executive coach, Hacia's purpose in society is to change workplace culture, ensuring diversity and inclusion are at the top of the agenda by promoting positive leadership. Recognising that change must come from the top down, her continued work and expertise in this area ensure that everyone can thrive.

"Understand the power of celebrating the smallest achievement."

"My success and ability to thrive came from harnessing everything within me and surrounding myself with supportive people and resources."

HOW TO
SURVIVE
AND
THRIVE
VOLUME II

KEVIN HINES

Storyteller, Author, and Filmmaker

Kevin Hines

I met Kevin during a Nugget Live Podcast and found his story to be one of the most fascinating I've ever heard. On 25 September, 2000, Kevin leapt off the Golden Gate Bridge. At only nineteen years of age, he survived a 250-foot drop, the equivalent of falling twenty-five stories at 75 mph in four seconds. This miracle alone is noteworthy, but what I found most poignant is how his story embodies the essence of the 'Survive and Thrive' series, celebrating the human condition, with its strength, tenacity, and determination to thrive.

Although Kevin was born in "squalor and abject poverty," he was given a second chance at life when he was adopted by parents who he describes as giving him "a beautiful life, childhood, and adolescence." Despite this idyllic new life, he describes how, at the age of seventeen, his "brain broke" and he began battling with mental health issues such as "paranoid delusions, hallucinations, auditory and visual mania, and even panic attacks." It was only when he suffered a "complete and total mental breakdown" on stage in front of 1200 people that he was diagnosed with bipolar disorder, the same "brain disease" that both of his biological parents suffered with, and therefore, something that he was "genetically predisposed to twice."

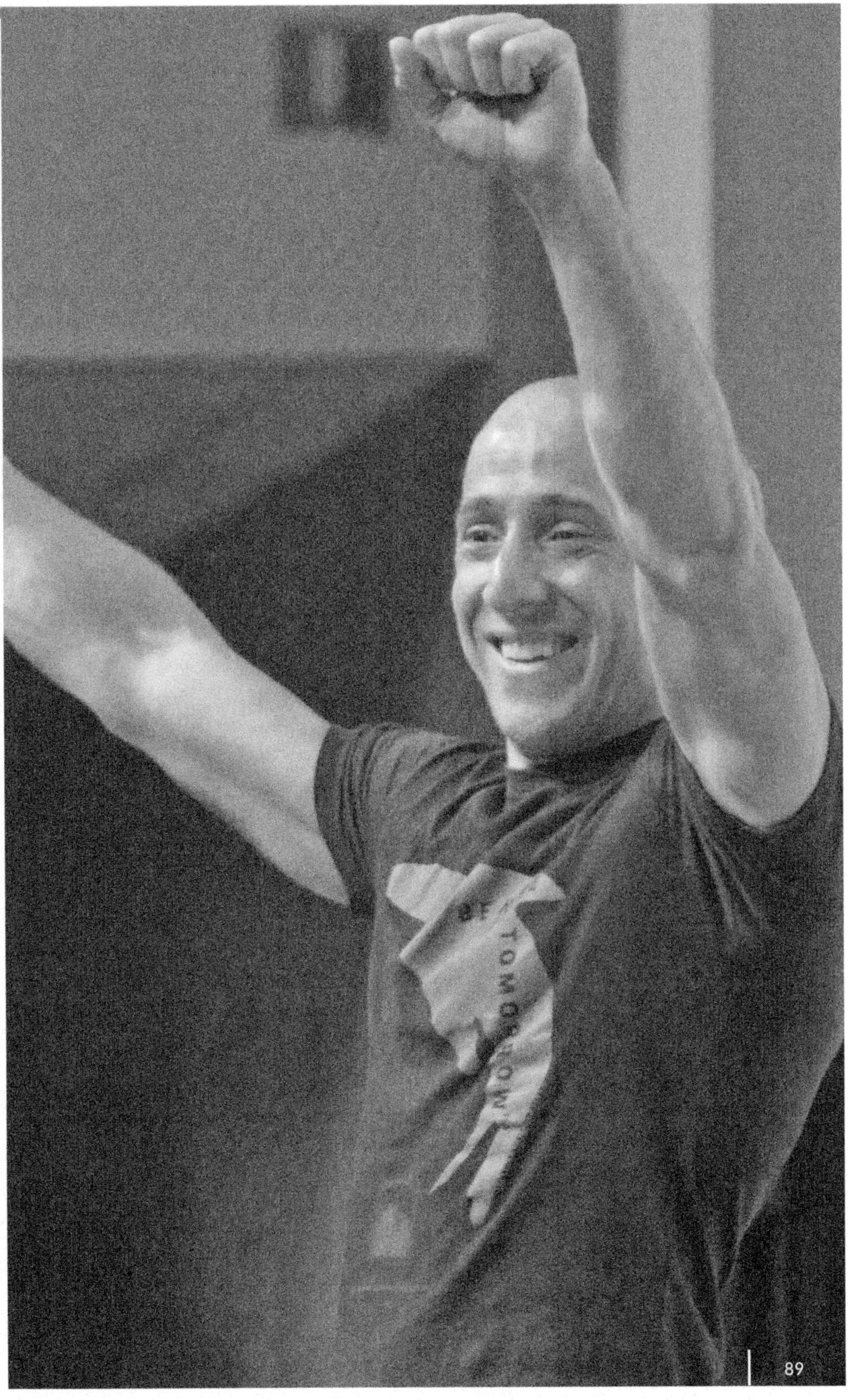

He describes his bipolar disorder poetically, recalling how he'd "skyrocket into this manic, euphoric natural high, caused by misaligned chemistry in the brain rather than any recreational drugs," before crashing "into a dark abyss of depression and psychosis," a cycle that happened for him on a weekly basis. By the time he'd reached the age of nineteen, his auditory hallucinations had become so severe that he was hearing voices in his head, telling him "I had to die, and that it was, in fact, inevitable." He highlights the difference between wanting to die and believing he "had to die."

Kevin had chosen to take his life in a way that was almost guaranteed, but what he realised in those few short seconds after falling was that he didn't actually want to die. In fact, he prayed to survive the fall, hitting the water with deadly impact. Although he was alive, he was drowning, but he was then miraculously saved by a sea lion, who kept him afloat until the Coast Guard arrived.

It's a story so impossible that it sounds like divine intervention, and he now uses this second chance at life to help others as a keynote speaker, openly discussing his mental health and how he's learned to manage it. He explains, "I wish I knew back then what I know today—that my thoughts don't have to become my actions. They can simply be my thoughts. They don't have to own, rule, or define what I do next."

"Keep going and do something good in this world."

After years of being in and out of psychiatric facilities, Kevin read an article in *Time* magazine on how to beat bipolar, depression, and other mental illnesses with a routine. He started exercising and soon found that it was making a huge difference to his physical and mental health, he began eating more healthily, with a specific focus on anti-inflammatory foods to support mental health; and he started going to therapy and learning more about his condition. Eventually, Kevin began to feel better.

Whilst he's learned to manage his bipolar disorder, he's reticent to declare that he's "recovered," preferring instead to say that he "lives in recovery every day." It's a constant fight for Kevin, who has, to date, been admitted to the psych ward on ten occasions. Yet each time he returns, he makes his exercise and healthy eating regime a top priority, and eventually, he regains enough health to be discharged.

It took Kevin a decade to reach a point of balance with his mental health; although he admits that he still suffers with symptoms such as mania, hallucinations, depression, paranoia, panic attacks, and anxiety, he takes proactive steps to "fight against them every single day." Research into his condition has led to Kevin developing a "science-backed ten-step guide" towards better brain health:

Therapy: Talking, art, music, blue light, and breathing therapy can be effective treatments.

Education: Learn more about your condition and share the information with your family and friends.

Exercise: Exercising for twenty-three minutes every day releases oxytocin in your brain, the hormone associated with love, trust, and relationship building.

Eat healthily: A balanced diet can improve your mood and sense of well-being. In particular, eating anti-inflammatory foods better balances your mind.

Coping strategies and mechanisms: Identify things you can do in your life that will help you help yourself to heal. It could be a hobby or staying away from negative influences.

Refraining from drugs and alcohol: These can impact your mental health negatively.

Advocate: By being truthful and sharing your experiences, you can actively advocate for yourself. By working towards changing public policy, you can advocate for others.

Meditation: Can help you recognise your inner peace and be calm.

Medication: Not all medication works for everyone, and it takes time to find the right course of treatment.

Mental health emergency plan: Write out and share a plan with family, friends, and professionals, which describes your symptoms, signs, and struggles.

This is a plan that helps Kevin manage his mental illness, and although he acknowledges that he still gets suicidal thoughts from time to time, he's resolute that he will never attempt to act on these thoughts ever again.

Whilst genetics are the main reason for Kevin's brain wiring, he has considered that there may have been other contributing factors to his poor mental health, such as his early start in life. He explains that he and his twin brother were "born in the worst neighbourhood in San Francisco, the Tenderloin District. We lived in and out of crack

Kevin Hines

"Mental health is the human rights issue of our time."

motels, the kind of places that you pay for by the hour. Our parents had no legal income, so they were, really, hustling to survive." Kevin's parents were using and selling drugs, and when their neglect was reported, the authorities "swooped us up and placed us into foster care." From then on, the two boys "bounced around from neglectful home to neglectful home," and unfortunately, his brother later died of bronchitis, a series of events that caused Kevin to become "detached from reality, developing abandonment issues that follow me to this day."

When he was adopted by Pat and Debi Hines, he felt as if he had been thrown a lifeline. With a new adopted family consisting of a black brother, white sister, and Irish/German parents, Kevin felt as though he had been "plucked from obscurity and given a future filled with care, love, and compassion." Despite all of this love, attention, and nurturing, all three siblings, each coming from different parents, with different experiences in life, experienced mental health breakdowns that put them all into psychiatric wards by the time they were thirty.

Kevin's adoptive father, Pat, had a similar start in life, as both of his parents died from alcoholism when he was still in high school. He was left with nothing but managed to put himself through college and become "one of the most prominent San Francisco bankers of his time." A rare individual, who sought to do good, Pat showered his adopted children with love and wonderful experiences. However, Kevin suggests that the damage inflicted on them as young children was so extreme and painful that no amount of nurturing could have reversed the effects of their trauma.

Having lived through two other attempted suicides before the Golden Gate Bridge attempt, Kevin is able to describe his emotional experiences sensitively and vividly. "You believe you're worthless. You believe you have no value. You believe you absolutely have nothing to live for. And you think you don't deserve to be on this earth, and you already feel that you are a burden to everybody who loves you. You feel that everybody who loves you actually hates you." The desperation is palpable, and his description allows us to understand why people who are suicidal may feel hopeless. Nevertheless, he states that "suicidal ideations are the greatest liars we know. We don't have to listen to them. That's the key."

It's taken Kevin decades to get to a point where he feels strong enough to help others whilst also helping himself. It's clear that his routine plays a major role in his ability to maintain balance in his life, and he is now able to recognise when he needs help and to seek support. Following his own advice, one of his coping strategies when having a suicidal episode is to look at himself in the mirror and remind himself of what he

"Your thoughts do not have to become your actions, they don't have to own, rule, or define what you do next! Make the choice to defy your thoughts if they don't serve you."

already knows: "My thoughts don't have to own rule or define what I do next."He will then reach out for help because he knows that his battle is a never-ending one. That help often comes from his wife and his parents, whom he regards as the real heroes in his story of surviving and thriving.

Kevin now spends the majority of his time educating people about mental health and, as a keynote speaker, he has raised "hundreds of millions of dollars in the past twenty-three years." The funds go towards making therapy free for individuals who are struggling with their mental health. It's clear that Kevin's focus is to uproot the stigma and create an open dialogue about mental health. His award-winning documentary, *Suicide, The Ripple* Effect "has been credited with saving over 1000 lives and counting, and has been seen by two million people in over twenty countries."

As a born storyteller, Kevin suggests that "stories are twenty-two times more effective and memorable than statistics or facts or PowerPoints." He explains that the exchange between storyteller and audience (regardless of the medium) causes "neural pathways to sync up so that the audience begins to feel empathy for the storyteller." Kevin is very proud of the lasting impact of his work. In twenty-three years, his videos have amassed over three billion views, with hundreds of thousands of people coming forward to claim that he has either saved or changed their lives in some way. Nevertheless, he sees himself as more of a "conduit" than a "lifesaver," explaining that whilst he delivers the message, it's the "people who go home and do the work; they're saving and changing their own lives."

Although he doesn't believe in coincidences, Kevin does believe in miracles. A year to the day that he jumped off the Golden Gate Bridge, he revisited the scene to drop a flower into the water and was met with a sea lion emerging from the water, a powerful reminder of what he'd survived.

He now knows eighteen people who have died by suicide and suggests that we need to find ways to "move forward through the pain, celebrate their lives, and honour their memories." For Kevin, one way of moving forward is to continue with his good work in helping others who struggle with their mental health, declaring, "I'm going to do this work until the day I die of natural causes."

"Yesterday is history, tomorrow is a mystery, today is a gift, that's why we call it the present, we all get to be here!"

HOW TO
SURVIVE
AND
THRIVE
VOLUME II

THE ART OF BEING BROKEN

HOW STORYTELLING SAVES LIVES

KEVIN HINES

DR. AKHTAR BADSHAH

Founder and Chief Catalyst of Catalytic Innovators Group, Distinguished Practitioner at the University of Washington, Author

Dr. Akhtar Badshah

A man of many talents with a profound passion for art, architecture, and technology, Akhtar has devoted his life to making a positive impact on others. His journey—from his early artwork and architectural projects to his philanthropic efforts—has led him from humble beginnings to engaging with some of the world's most influential figures. As a sports shoe designer and founder of an iconic brand, I admire Akhtar's approach to embracing new opportunities and pushing beyond his comfort zone to achieve the extraordinary. Although our paths differ, we share a common entrepreneurial spirit and a deep understanding of our purpose.

Born in India to a "not traditional or ritual-bound, middle-class family," Akhtar's life took a turn when his parents separated at the age of seven. The transition from a typical family flat to a modest two-room flat was challenging, as his mother had to work to make ends meet.

103

"If we could just be ourselves,
then we would learn to
appreciate each other."

As an "awkward, lanky kid," Akhtar had to step in to support his family—not by earning money but by handling everyday tasks while attending school. He would grocery shop, negotiate with the butcher, and run out in the morning to buy butter or milk. These responsibilities forced him to grow up quickly and ignited an entrepreneurial spirit as he learned how to negotiate.

After five years apart, Akhtar's parents reconciled and the family moved back to Mumbai. Akhtar joined a new school, though he admits, "I didn't enjoy studying in the traditional fashion of memorising everything and then getting tested; it didn't suit my sensibilities." However, he discovered a passion for art, which remains a significant part of his life today. Akhtar's mother, a talented artist, nurtured his creativity, and he was inspired by his uncle, one of India's most accomplished modern artists.

Akhtar was also deeply interested in technology, and he combined this with his passion for art by applying to one of the most prestigious architecture schools in the country. There, his creativity, technological curiosity, and entrepreneurial spirit converged, allowing him to truly thrive. He states, "You are either going to go to work or you're going to start an architectural practice, so you've got to have entrepreneurial skills."

Although the learning process was both challenging and rewarding for Akhtar's development, it ultimately transformed his approach to architecture. After five years of rigorous study, he secured an internship in Sri Lanka, where he had the opportunity to work with the prestigious architect Geoffry Bawa at the Sri Lankan Parliament complex. Reflecting on this experience, he explains, "That's when I learned, in a very profound way, what architecture is all about."

For Akhtar, architecture is "a deep engagement with physical space, nature, people, economics, and geography." Although he had to return to school after his internship to complete his final year, his passion for working and earning remained strong. So, when the chance to join a firm came along, he eagerly accepted. At the firm, he played a key role in a project in Riyadh, a large-scale endeavour that included designing the headquarters for the government, mayor, and police. The firm rapidly expanded from a small team of two to seventy employees in just a few weeks.

Akhtar suggests, "It was at that point that I really learned how to work. Starting with nothing, I memorised drawings, hired structural engineers, mechanical engineers, and every other expert who needed to be brought in." He was also attending school and had actually hired one of the faculty members as the lead structural engineer on his project.

He vividly describes this exciting chapter of his life. "I was there 24/7, literally sleeping in the office. We were all young, smoking, living off junk food, sleeping on foam mattresses, and just working." During this intense period, Akhtar discovered his true strengths—motivating others and getting people to deliver results. This philosophy became the "genesis" of his life. He explains, "Work is not just work; it's about how you show up. You don't need to be an expert on everything as long as you decide to show up."

Akhtar reflects that for most of his life, he has embraced the power of saying yes and encourages others to "do something that you may not necessarily feel very comfortable with." He also suggests shifting the focus from "What's in it for me?" to asking, "Is this extending the common good? Does what I do contribute to making our planet a better place?"

Akhtar was raised in an India that was increasingly Westernised. He attended an English-speaking Catholic school and has spent much of his life in America. Despite these influences, he credits India with teaching him the value of authenticity. "India is not one group of people; it's incredibly diverse and different," he says, reflecting on how this diversity shaped his understanding of staying true to oneself and having the confidence to be yourself.

By his late twenties, Akhtar was teaching on the Aga Khan Program for Islamic Architecture' at the Massachusetts Institute of Technology, where he graduated with a master's degree and a PhD. This role presented a new challenge, as he quickly realised that teaching wasn't just about imparting knowledge—it was about understanding what you can contribute and earning the recognition, respect, and attention of your students on a daily basis.

He eventually transitioned into the non-profit sector to focus on issues facing megacities, first moving to New York and later to Seattle. However, when an earthquake struck India, Akhtar felt compelled to get involved. Drawing on his leadership skills and experience mobilising people, he spearheaded fundraising efforts and successfully raised $1 million—an impressive sum at the time.

This experience ignited Akhtar's interest in becoming part of an NGO called Digital Partners, which focused on bridging the digital divide. Although he initially had limited knowledge of the subject, he saw it as "a matter of understanding where you can make a difference." His ability to bring people together, take ideas, and "put them to fruition" allowed him to "get things done." Given that this was in the early 2000s, the initiative garnered significant attention from organisations like the United Nations. Akhtar explains, "We were accessing the rich tech diaspora communities and motivating them to share their acumen and knowledge with

"Nobody has learned how to walk without falling down."

their home countries." Even Kofi Annan, the UN Secretary-General, hosted Digital Partners at their conventions, highlighting the impact and relevance of their work. Akthar was able to "bring the private sector, the non-profit sector, the academic sector, and the community together around an issue, and for the first time, create these multi-sectorial partnerships."

The success of the NGO eventually led Akhtar to oversee Microsoft's corporate philanthropy for a decade. During this time, he spearheaded the launch of two major programs: Unlimited Potential and Youth Spark. The first initiative established 70,000 community technology learning centres across 103 countries. This was a remarkable achievement, especially given the locations of these centres, ranging from the jungles of Indonesia to the mountains of Latin America and the deserts of the Middle East. As Akhtar notes, it represented a massive infusion of technology into some of the most remote and underserved areas. The second initiative centred on equipping young people with technical skills, aiming to open doors to higher education and career opportunities while fostering their entrepreneurial spirit. The program was designed to empower them to become job creators rather than just job seekers. As Akhtar explains, "Today, many of these individuals are working with advanced AI, demonstrating the long-term impact of the training."

He reflects on how his career has evolved in three distinct phases, with each decade dedicated to a different focus: architecture, non-profit work, and corporate philanthropy at Microsoft. Now in his fourth decade since leaving education, Akhtar is pursuing multiple endeavours, including teaching, writing books, and leading workshops on finding purpose. He marvels at his journey, reflecting on how he went from "growing up on the streets of Mumbai, playing pick-up cricket" to working for some of the wealthiest individuals in the world and interacting with some of the most influential people globally.

As the Head of Corporate Philanthropy at Microsoft, he managed the company's global philanthropy portfolio, including employee giving and volunteer programs. He suggests that companies have four things they can bring to community investment.

1. A service or product. In Microsoft's case, it's technology.
2. People with talent who can give their time, talent, and treasure.
3. Financial resources, at whatever scale the company decides.
4. Advocacy. Microsoft's technology empowers people.

Akthar learned that, by strategically combining all four elements "in a planned, consistent way, the difference you could make in the world would be exponential." He believed his approach was far more effective than writing a cheque, organising volunteer efforts, or donating items. He explains, "We were able to unleash all aspects of the company's power for the greater good."

As the co-founder of Purpose Mindset, Akthar has reached over 5000 people worldwide, ranging from children in rural India to students in Egypt, CEOs, ministers, deans, and NGO leaders. For Akthar, this work is deeply fulfilling: "It's incredibly enriching because many people have never actually taken the time to reflect on their purpose. Doing so in a group setting opens up rich connections and breaks down barriers."

Purpose Mindset's impact extends beyond individuals, helping organisations articulate their purpose statements. Akthar has observed that while companies often know their mission, vision, and values, they rarely address the fundamental question: "Why do you exist?" He suggests, "A single, well-crafted statement can make a huge difference, helping people find meaning in what they do, both personally and through their work. It's not just about crafting a statement; Akthar's purpose and mission go further—to shift mindsets and help people focus on the positive instead of the negative. True value lies in empowering others to thrive. To achieve this, he encourages people to recognise those moments when they feel inspired, creative, intellectually engaged, or motivated. This process, which he refers to as a "purpose skill," helps people identify their strengths and align them with their purpose, enabling them to overcome negative thoughts.

"Purpose is your 'why.' It goes beyond the 'what' and the 'how.'"

His advice is: "Use your values, use your strengths, use your purpose, and visualise it; this will allow you to build muscle that will lead to change." From the beginning, it's been clear that Akthar's purpose has always been to make a positive impact on the lives of others. Whether through his innovative work in architecture, his dedicated philanthropic endeavours or his commitment to helping individuals discover and live their purpose, his actions are driven by a deep-seated desire to contribute to the greater good.

Despite being a multifaceted, multi-talented individual, Akthar's guiding philosophy is strikingly simple: "A life full of meaning brings fulfilment and contentment." Akthar understands that true fulfilment doesn't come from external achievements alone but from aligning one's actions with a more profound sense of purpose. It's this alignment that brings lasting satisfaction, allowing people to succeed and do so in a way that feels authentic and rewarding. For Akthar, the greatest reward is witnessing the transformation in others as they begin to live more meaningful and purpose-driven lives. This simple yet profound philosophy is the foundation of his life's work and continues to drive him forwards.

"Don't say no. Seize the opportunities that come to you."

HOW TO
SURVIVE
AND
THRIVE
VOLUME II

DR. AMINE AREZKI, MBA

CMO to Watch 2024, TEDx and Keynote Speaker, Visionary Leader and Strategic Executor, B2B Strategic Marketing Director

Dr. Amine Arezki, MBA

As CEO of Reebok, I often approached challenges as opportunities—a mindset that Dr. Arezki and I share. Like me, Amine is a natural problem-solver with a deep passion for marketing. His focus on both design and technology has led to the creation of several life-changing products. From a challenging start in life, he has risen to the top of his field as an innovative designer, living and working in four different countries around the world.

Originally from Algeria, Amine grew up quickly amidst the challenges of a turbulent ten-year period during his adolescence. While he may have missed aspects of a typical childhood due to these circumstances, he believes he gained something far more valuable: the ability to survive and navigate complex situations. He learned whom to trust, where to go, what to say, when to stay silent, and how to find a solution to a problem.

Dr. Arezki's parents were both dedicated professionals, which placed them in a difficult position during Algeria's period of uncertainty. Amine explains that during this time, certain groups were resistant to change. If you were a journalist, professor, teacher, or doctor—any role associated with an open mind or science—you could face challenges. He adds, "My parents, with their commitment to development and knowledge, were seen as different by these groups."

Amine's father was a professor of neurology, and his mother was a physiotherapist with her own business and a former national basketball player and team captain. During this period, both faced pressures related to their professions. As a young boy, Amine could sense the anxiety within his family. Realising he could either contribute to this fear or remain calm, he chose to focus on his studies and excel in school. Although he found school too theoretical, maintaining a sense of normalcy amidst the chaos became his priority.

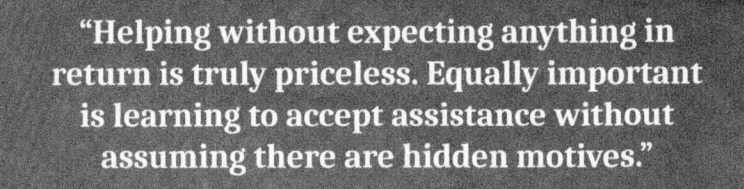

"Helping without expecting anything in return is truly priceless. Equally important is learning to accept assistance without assuming there are hidden motives."

At the same time, Amine suggests that the isolation he experienced allowed him to explore interests outside of school. While he missed out on typical childhood activities like practising sports in a club, going to the cinema, and hanging out with friends, he turned to learning languages, music, and art. This period taught him a valuable lesson: the ability to educate himself independently and think creatively, skills he continues to embrace today.

These ten years cast a shadow over Amine's upbringing, and he recalls waking up each morning to hear news of families nearby facing. There was a particular instance when his father narrowly avoided a difficult situation at the hospital where he worked. Nevertheless, Amine's family worked hard to protect him from their circumstances and maintained a positive attitude and outlook, which he compares to Roberto Benigni's film *Life is Beautiful* (1997). In fact, it was not until much later in life that Amine learned of the stories about his father's close encounters with danger. Reflecting on those times, Amine notes, "In the midst of it all, you might think it's normal, but looking back, it was an incredibly challenging situation."

Amine readily acknowledges that he thrives on staying busy. Fortunately, with two working parents in professional roles who were dedicated to supporting and protecting their families, he had access to most of what he needed. Nevertheless, Amine's introduction to mathematics, physics, programming, and robotics came relatively late, as he initially focused on art, music, and other creative pursuits. However, he explains the vital connection between these fields, noting how creativity enhances science by "extrapolating it into technology, marketing, new business models, and beyond."

"There's always a solution to a problem, just keep searching."

When the conflict ended in 2002, Amine was still pursuing his engineering degree. He then shifted his focus and joined a robotics club led by an inspirational and forward-thinking professor who had studied in England. Together, they founded an association and began competing with teams and nations from around the world.

The competition was held annually, with each year presenting a new set of challenges, such as "getting a ball into a specific hole at a certain speed." Amine discovered he thoroughly enjoyed the problem-solving aspect of the process. He explains, "You had clear objectives, and you had to think creatively to find a technical solution." Thriving in this environment, Amine leveraged his creativity and scientific skills to tackle problems through teamwork. Despite a limited budget, his team achieved notable success, advancing from the quarter-finals to the semi-finals and ultimately reaching the final.

After a period of stagnation, Amine experienced a time "when everything was booming." This momentum helped him to earn his Master's in Robotics and Intelligent Systems from Pierre and Marie Curie University, with a scholarship exchange at Rutgers University in New Jersey.

While in America, Amine worked on a series of "very interesting topics," primarily focusing on applying robotics to motivate and rehabilitate stroke patients through games. Although he was originally scheduled to stay for just nine months, he quickly settled in, met his wife, Anusch, and ended up staying for two years. The couple would have remained longer, but they chose to return to Europe to be closer to the family.

While living in Paris, Amine and Anusch decided to pursue their PhDs, Anusch in chemistry and Amine in robotics. Simultaneously, Amine aimed to develop a startup around his research. He was deeply involved in all aspects of the venture, including product development, marketing, and business strategy. However, despite his significant contributions, Dr. Arezki was blindsided when his senior associate declined to include Amine's name on the patent.

This situation understandably led to conflict. It wasn't just about receiving recognition for his work; financial issues related to intellectual property rights also came into play. The strained working relationship made it evident that continuing was untenable. With a heavy heart, Amine decided to leave his PhD program and take up a paid position with a multinational corporation.

At this pivotal moment, Amine received a lifeline: the chance to continue his PhD while working. After four years, he earned his PhD in Robotics from UVSQ Université de Versailles Saint-Quentin-en-Yvelines. Although his research focus had shifted

"I'd rather do things and fail than regret not even trying."

from his earlier work, it remained equally compelling. His new research centred on understanding human behaviour in public spaces like airports and train stations. The goal was to develop robots that could assist people based on their motion and speed, enabling the system to detect if someone is lost, seeking information, in danger, or rushing, and providing appropriate support. He explains, "It was a very interesting topic because it involved building a mobile robot capable of interacting with people."

Balancing work, family, and his PhD research was intense, but Amine valued the experience as a significant learning curve. He notes, "I learned how to juggle multiple tasks simultaneously and manage my time effectively." When it came time for his presentation, Amine prepared thoroughly, crafting slides, animations, and more. Facing a jury of four, he was uncertain of what to expect. Ultimately, he was pleased with the result, sharing, "They appreciated the topic, the clarity of the writing, and the practical application of the work. It wasn't just theoretical or simulated; it was applied science, and I received the highest grade." His achievements didn't stop there; recently, Amine was also awarded Student of the Year by the London Business School during his Executive MBA, as well as earning a spot on the top 100 Worldwide Executive MBA ranking by Poets and Qants and Chief Marketing Officer to Watch 2024 by CMO Alliance.

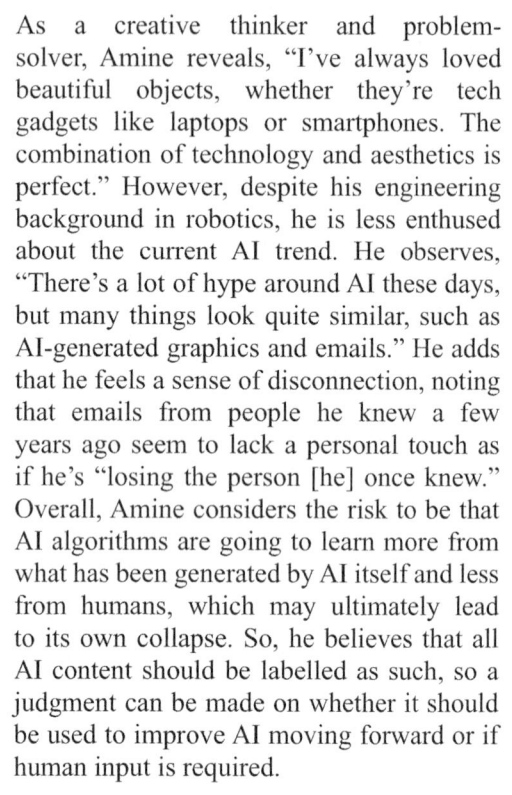

As a creative thinker and problem-solver, Amine reveals, "I've always loved beautiful objects, whether they're tech gadgets like laptops or smartphones. The combination of technology and aesthetics is perfect." However, despite his engineering background in robotics, he is less enthused about the current AI trend. He observes, "There's a lot of hype around AI these days, but many things look quite similar, such as AI-generated graphics and emails." He adds that he feels a sense of disconnection, noting that emails from people he knew a few years ago seem to lack a personal touch as if he's "losing the person [he] once knew." Overall, Amine considers the risk to be that AI algorithms are going to learn more from what has been generated by AI itself and less from humans, which may ultimately lead to its own collapse. So, he believes that all AI content should be labelled as such, so a judgment can be made on whether it should be used to improve AI moving forward or if human input is required.

Although he is invested in AI, Amine is concerned about its potential to replace jobs and make processes faster and cheaper at the expense of human connection. He argues, "Society needs to consider radical changes in how wealth is generated and how people earn a living." He advocates for AI and robotics to "serve and support" rather than merely replace, calling for an "economic disruption that must be addressed urgently and taken very seriously." He expands this view in his work with autonomous trains, trains run by AI, which support rather than replace the driver.

"Think simple and think creatively, and focus on the real target."

Given Amine's background, it's no surprise that he envisions a world where robots handle all the work, allowing people more time to enjoy life. Recently featured in the prestigious French magazine *Paris Match* for his work on autonomous trains aimed at enhancing mobility for a growing population, Amine clearly stands out as a multi-faceted innovator. He seamlessly blends his passions for technology, design, and marketing to drive meaningful advancements.

As a keynote speaker, Amine has participated in numerous events, and the magic of networking has given him "the most valuable experiences beyond work and family because they involve connecting with people, sharing ideas, and listening." In fact, the connections he made during the Musa Tariq Zoom call led to a collaboration on the *Mask for All Together* initiative, which produced masks during the COVID-19 pandemic. He explains, "The name emerged from our discussions and brainstorming sessions. We handled everything from the final design and distribution to finding sponsors and sourcing filament." Amine is rightfully proud of this achievement, reflecting,

Photo - Christian Kammer

"This is something I will remember for a lifetime. It was a chance to contribute to a charitable cause, connect with like-minded individuals, and create something that, hopefully, saved lives."

Today, Dr. Arezki is working to integrate all his passions and patents: creativity, robotics, AI, and marketing. He is also leveraging his love of sports to develop a virtual advertising platform aimed at making a positive impact. MarkaMotion is an innovative and unique virtual advertising platform that integrates AR dynamic ads onto sports jerseys. As the founder, he explains, "Our invention is revolutionising the way brands advertise and engage with fans in the world of sports. With our technology, clubs and broadcasters can display targeted, changeable advertisements on players' shirts during broadcasts, maximising sponsorship value and viewer engagement and providing analytics and performance tracking for sponsors.

He's also keen to point out that the project is mostly focused on helping sports clubs improve their financial situation and helping smaller brands gain visibility at major events where they would otherwise be overlooked. He states, "We make your virtual logos, messages, and media visible on selected sports jerseys, broadcasted and targeting your preferred region. This innovative approach enhances fan engagement and provides new revenue streams for teams and broadcasters."

"Regret is a feeling I'm not
comfortable with; therefore,
I do not set any limits on myself."

HOW TO SURVIVE AND THRIVE
VOLUME II

Let's share wisdom!

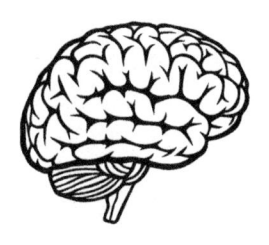

"Have a focus and a passion."

Dr. Gerry Curatola
Biologic Dentist & Wellness Pioneer

"The more you do to help someone else be successful, the more successful you will become."

Dayna Steele
Rock Radio Hall of Famer

"As a speaker, know your audience, incorporate stories, and have a compelling conclusion or call to action."

David Doerrier
Founder of Present Your Way To Success

"Your life story is your leadership story."

Douglas Conant
Business Leader

"Nothing holds more weight than combining your passion with authentic excitement and professional services."

David Forman
Founder of Mastermind

"Embrace the curiosity about your differences and celebrate impact and success together."

David Homan
Founder and CEO of Orchestrated Connecting

"Have gratitude; be grateful that you're doing the things you chose to do and that you've woken up every morning and can do them."

Dominique Wright
CEO and Founder of FAND

"If you have sunshine in your soul, you'll always be happy. Then, you need to spread the happiness to other people."

Doru Borsan
Business Leader

"Take time to feel what you're going through."

Elena Armijo
Executive and Leadership Coach

"When life is falling apart, get
rid of what's not important."

Dustin Siggins
Founder of Proven Media Solutions

"Strength lies in mastering your thoughts,
not in controlling the world around you."

David Torres Mora
Head of Brand at One Golden Nugget

"Sometimes you just have to take that leap of faith.
Progress doesn't come from the comfort zone."

Ekaterina Volskaya
Talk Show Host & Web3 Enthusiast

"When our purpose leads,
possibilities multiply."

Eleni Kitra
Founder and CEO of KITRA INCLUSIVE

"Figure out what success looks like for you. It has to fit into the lifestyle you want. That's the beauty of entrepreneurship."

Evin Schwartz
CEO and Founder of Belouga

"Keep everything customer-centric. If you're not providing what you're promising to your users, you'll know very quickly."

Forrest Smith
CEO and Co-founder of Kineon

"Don't think about how it should be; accept how life is."

Gastón Corbala
Founder and CEO of The Backpackster

"If you have a goal and you're wondering how to do it, just take that leap of faith and follow through on it."

Francois Hewing
Founder of MegNivicent Money

"Assume positive intent and give people the benefit of the doubt. It can transform how we communicate, collaborate, and build relationships."

Elizabeth Birch
Vice President of Customer Experience at Visiting Media

"Alignment eats strategy for breakfast."

George Alifragis
Senior Vice President at Metropolitan Partners Group

"Network constantly because you never know when you will need your network."

Greg Muzzillo
Founder of Proforma

"Finding your authentic self is hard work. It can be emotional, vulnerable, and sometimes scary. But it's worthwhile because it brings about who you are, what you want, and how you want to see and go through the world."

Hillary Schoninger
Psychotherapist

"The most important relationship you have is the one you have with yourself."

Hiten Bhatt
Founder of Be Great Training

"Every day, my puppy, Stanley, wakes up excited for the day. Be more Stanley."

Hayley Meakes
Mindset Coach

"When you are starting a company, you need to be pointing to evidence when you are iterating because the goal of any Start-Up is to iterate as quickly as humanly possible."

Harrison Telyan
Co-Founder of NUMI

"Life gives you a blank canvas every day. Make sure you fill it with as many colours as possible."

Ipek Williamson
Transition Coach

"When you are in the process of developing discipline, it doesn't particularly feel good. But once you have it as part of your mindset, it will bring you comfort and relaxation."

Ivan Illán
Author

"Focus on this minute right now. Take a step in the right direction. Then another, and another. Push yourself to make decisions and act."

Jack Doueck
Principal and Founder of Advanced Energy Capital

"All success comes as a by-product of pursuing self-mastery. When you can learn to trust in your ability to think, plan, and act, not much will evade your grasp."

Jackson Millan
Wealth Mentor

"Pause and ask yourself what you need to move forward and make it work."

Jeanette Bronée
Keynote Speaker, Author, and Culture Strategist

"Keep things in perspective. What really matters, and what do you really care about?"

Jeff Bogensberger
Founder and CEO of The Laughing Otter

CARLA BERBARY

Speaker, Therapist and University Tutor

Carla Berbary

Both Carla and I grew up against the backdrop of war. For me, it was World War II, but I remember still having a carefree childhood despite the constant threat of bombs being dropped over Manchester, ten miles away from my home. Similarly, Carla spent her most formative years in Lebanon during the fifteen-year civil war, and she too has "happy memories" of that time in her life. Although Carla's family was based well within the firing line, perhaps both of our experiences are a testament to the resilience of the childhood spirit, which pays little heed to the upheavals of life and instead focuses on the joy.

Carla was born in Lebanon at the start of the civil war and spent her first fifteen years in a war that displaced nearly one million people out of a population of around three million. As a child, she did not appear to experience the trauma of being potentially targeted by a sniper, bombed, or rushing to the bunkers with the rest of the civilians, as bomber planes flew above. However, looking back as an adult, she can appreciate that her naivety protected her from the horrible reality in which she was living. It wasn't until she began reading books about that part of Lebanon's history that she became retrospectively petrified of what she had experienced as a child, an event that resulted in around 150,000 fatalities. It's no surprise that she learned early on that "life is not guaranteed."

"A smile for some people will
be the only smile they get that
day or even that week."

The details of living in a perpetual state of conflict are quite compelling. As a child, Carla would accompany her friends to the bunkers for safety, then scour the rubble post-bombing for the expended shellings. She remembers her lounge area being decorated with "two or three 70 cm tall rocket shells," used as vases for lilies from their garden. It's clear that Carla's experiences have given her an appreciation for the fragility of life, as she states, "Life was valuable and time was valuable." It's an awareness that has remained with her and something many overlook. She instructs, "Never take time for granted."

Carla looks back in awe at former teachers, who put their lives at risk to protect students during bombing raids. She recalls one teacher in particular telling "silly, funny stories" to distract the children as they hid from bombs flying overhead. At the age of eleven, Carla took it all for granted, perhaps because she had not known any different. Today, when she reflects on the heroism of the teachers at her Catholic school, she is convinced that it taught her something significant: "Most of the time we can support each other, and whatever we can support with, we need to do it."

"Use the right lens when looking at people."

Interestingly, Carla identifies our unique fingerprints as a visual metaphor: "We come to life to leave a fingerprint, and so we can't not utilise what we were given." In other words, whatever unique way we can help people, we need to be willing to do so. For Carla, it was her ability to listen. It may seem simple, but the art of listening is not something that comes easy to many. However, she expresses that "listening to people and supporting them was something that I really enjoyed."

Although she may have taken growing up during a civil war in her stride, Carla's domestic situation was to have a more long-lasting effect on her. She explains, "My father was abusive to my mother, and now I understand that there was also abuse towards us four girls because the best gift you can give your daughter is to treat her mother well." Much like her childlike naivety towards the war, Carla was not fully aware of the reality of the situation. Her mother suffered from mental health issues, and her father, who was both physically and emotionally abusive towards his wife, "used it to position himself as the victim." Believing her father's misery was directly a cause of her mother affected her relationship with both parents, as she explains, "I hated my mother…and thought my father's happiness was in my hands." As she grew older, the emotional abuse took its toll, and Carla became suicidal at the age of thirteen. Even at such a young age, she knew she was responsible for turning things around, and after changing schools and trying to work on her own mental health, things started to become more positive.

As she grew into a young woman, she became closer to her mother, and their relationship flourished when Carla was studying at university. They became confidantes, and as Carla's newfound understanding of her mother grew, so did her love and respect. But tragically, five days after her first child was born, Carla's world was shattered when she learned of her mother's sudden death. An event that's still raw and arresting fifteen years later, it is perhaps magnified by Carla's perception of wasted opportunities and all of the things left unsaid.

After obtaining a bachelor's degree in computer science, Carla found her true passion and went back to university to retrain in psychology. It was during this time that she noticed the most effective teachers were not necessarily the most skilled but the ones that were able to connect with their students. It occurred to her that "people may forget what you did, but they will never forget how you made them feel, the good *and* the bad."

It was at this point that she ditched the programming part and retrained in psychology, believing she had a true talent and vocation for helping people in this way. She also notes that before she had any training, her friends used to call her 'the psychologist,' pre-empting her destiny in a way, to listen and use her innate talent for helping others. Today, she is a therapist in a private practice and a teacher at university. She has dedicated herself to helping people navigate trauma, grief, and loss, and specialises in providing support to victims of narcissistic abuse.

Carla's job requires an element of inner strength, resilience and determination, and it's clear that she has an abundance of all these qualities. Her father calls her a "risk-taker," while she prefers to call herself "adventurous." She taught herself to drive a car and swim, even though she wasn't allowed near water, and she left the family home in Lebanon to settle down in Australia, where she resides now. She's also had her fair share of trauma, which makes her an empathetic listener.

As a public speaker, Carla leads workshops and seminars in both the corporate and academic worlds. She also runs programmes for students on a variety of helpful subjects; for example, she runs a programme to reduce the use of vaping amongst teenagers. Her role as a university lecturer in counselling is rewarding for several reasons.

In the teaching/learning dynamic, she suggests that students "come from different perspectives that I had never thought of, so this opens up my mind to new ways of looking at things." Furthermore, the aspect of connection is one of great importance. If what she says can resonate with a student, or if she can connect with them on a deeper level, "that's what I'm after."

Her podcast, Not a Life Sentence, invites guest speakers to share their experiences to highlight the latest research surrounding mental health. Anything from a chat with Housewife of Dubai Caroline Stanbury and her husband, former Real Madrid player Sergio Carrallo, to midlife crises, chakra dancing, and even going from $16 an hour to a five-figure monthly income. The mind is a fragile cornucopia of thoughts and processes that needs exploration, and Carla's podcast aims to promote the idea that we are not stuck; we can thrive and not just survive.

Listening to people's trauma on a daily basis is not easy, and Carla is keen to point out that "self-care in [their] industry is not a luxury; it's a necessity." Because of this, she makes sure to take regular time off by either going on holiday or taking time out to train and upskill. She is also professionally bound to discuss her cases with her clinical supervisor as a sort of talking therapy to ensure mental well-being.

"Little changes can make a big difference in your life."

"Your skills are to be shared. You're not allowed to keep them to yourself."

What she really attempts to do in all her endeavours is to give people a voice, either through her therapy sessions, advocating for the discipline of counselling, or her podcasts. She explains, "My mum had the biggest impact on my life because she was the underdog. She tried to protect herself, but she couldn't, and she tried to protect us... My mum didn't have a voice." Now, as an adult, she can identify how similar she is to her mother, both sharing that same sense of resilience, the same curiosity (her mother was taken out of school against her will at the age of eleven), and the same sense of compassion. Regardless of her early estrangement from her mother, it is their special bond in Carla's adulthood that remains. Her mother lives on in Carla and in the work that she does. With certainty, if she were here today, Carla's mum would be proud of her daughter's achievements, proud of her value system, and proud of her attitude towards life and events. But, most of all, she would be proud of the little girl who grew up to be her best friend.

"We don't know what
people are going through,
so be kind."

HOW TO
SURVIVE
AND
THRIVE
VOLUME II

NICK AND MELISSA STEHR

Directors of HLS Healthcare

Nick and Melissa Stehr

I know what it's like to have a superpower in the guise of a wife and business partner and how much fun it can be working together. Nick and Melissa, a power couple, married for twenty-nine years and running their healthcare company together for the past seventeen years, have demonstrated how effective a shared purpose can be when mixed with passion, hard work, and tenacity.

Nick grew up in Sydney in a single-parent household after his parents divorced when he was just two years old. When his mother remarried, Nick found himself with two father figures. He fondly recalls how his German stepfather became a significant part of their lives, saying, "He was someone really special to me and my brother. He treated us like his own and had a big impact on our lives."

"Everything that happens is an opportunity to learn something and adapt for the better."

During school holidays, Nick and his brother would travel to Queensland to visit their father. To a young Nick, his life seemed glamorous—he was a swimming coach who lived "in a penthouse by the river." So, captivated by this lifestyle and wanting to live with his father, Nick decided at sixteen to fly across Australia and join his dad.

However, the day he arrived, Nick's dad sat him down and broke the news that he was getting remarried for the third time and had arranged for Nick to live with his grandmother instead. Having flown all that way and excited to spend time with his father, he learned that his new wife's children would be moving into the penthouse, and there was no room for Nick.

Although the rejection stung, Nick found comfort in his grandmother's home, where he truly felt loved. Nevertheless, the hurt he felt derailed him, leading him to fall in with the wrong crowd in high school, and it wasn't until a fateful meeting with his soulmate, Melissa, that his life took a turn for the better, setting him on a new, more positive path.

Nick met Melissa during his final year at high school. And the following year, unplanned, they quickly became pregnant with their son Tyler, and "life took a pretty sharp turn" for the young couple. Melissa and Nick, now parents at eighteen years old, focused on "putting food on the table." His own experiences coloured his attitude to fatherhood; as Nick explains, "I wanted to be a father who's present; I wanted to be around for my boys."

"You've got to be willing to do whatever it takes."

For Melissa, getting pregnant at seventeen was initially a terrifying experience. She recalls how she "didn't tell Nick until [she] was four and a half months pregnant." To her immense relief and happiness, Nick was overjoyed by the news. Her parents, however, were less than pleased. Her mother, who had once been in the same situation, pregnant at a young age with her son taken away for adoption, was especially disappointed at first. But Melissa was determined that history would not repeat itself. She remembers thinking, "I'm a mum, and I'm not letting anyone take my baby."

Nick describes this time as a "pivotal moment in our lives." Despite not having wealthy families to support them, they were determined to give their child the best possible opportunities. He was resolute in not becoming just another statistic, so he and Melissa worked tirelessly to provide for their growing family. Melissa, in particular, was "an incredible mother" who never had the luxury of being a stay-at-home mum because they simply couldn't afford it. Nick recalls how she had to return to work soon after giving birth.

Through their childhood experiences, the couple had developed their own sense of tenacity and making the best out of situations. Determined to create a "life that we'd be proud of," the couple got married.

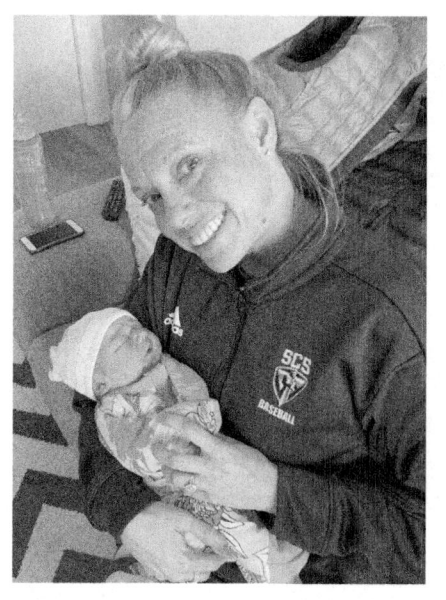

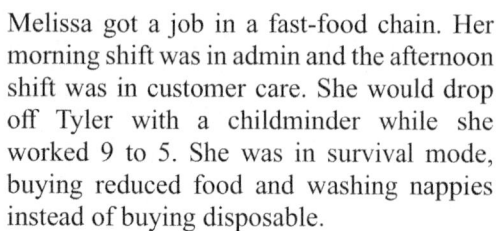

Melissa got a job in a fast-food chain. Her morning shift was in admin and the afternoon shift was in customer care. She would drop off Tyler with a childminder while she worked 9 to 5. She was in survival mode, buying reduced food and washing nappies instead of buying disposable.

As a teenage mother, Melissa's life became quite isolating. While her friends were out enjoying themselves, Melissa was either working or at home caring for her young son. Reflecting on that time, she admits, "It was quite lonely from my perspective." Fortunately, after the initial shock and worry, Melissa's parents became her support network, with her mother, a "very strong woman," acting as her mentor and guide.

After a few years of taking on odd jobs, Nick decided to work for a gas pipeline construction company, primarily because the pay was good. The job required him to leave his family and live in central Queensland, but as he explains, "It enabled us to earn some reasonable money, so we no longer had to beg, borrow, and steal just to buy groceries." Eventually, Melissa and their son, Tyler, joined Nick, and the family lived together in a caravan. Despite the challenges, there was a sense that they were finally "moving forward."

Things changed dramatically for Nick when he went to Sydney to visit his mother. During the visit, they had lunch with a friend of hers, who weeks later offered Nick a sales job in

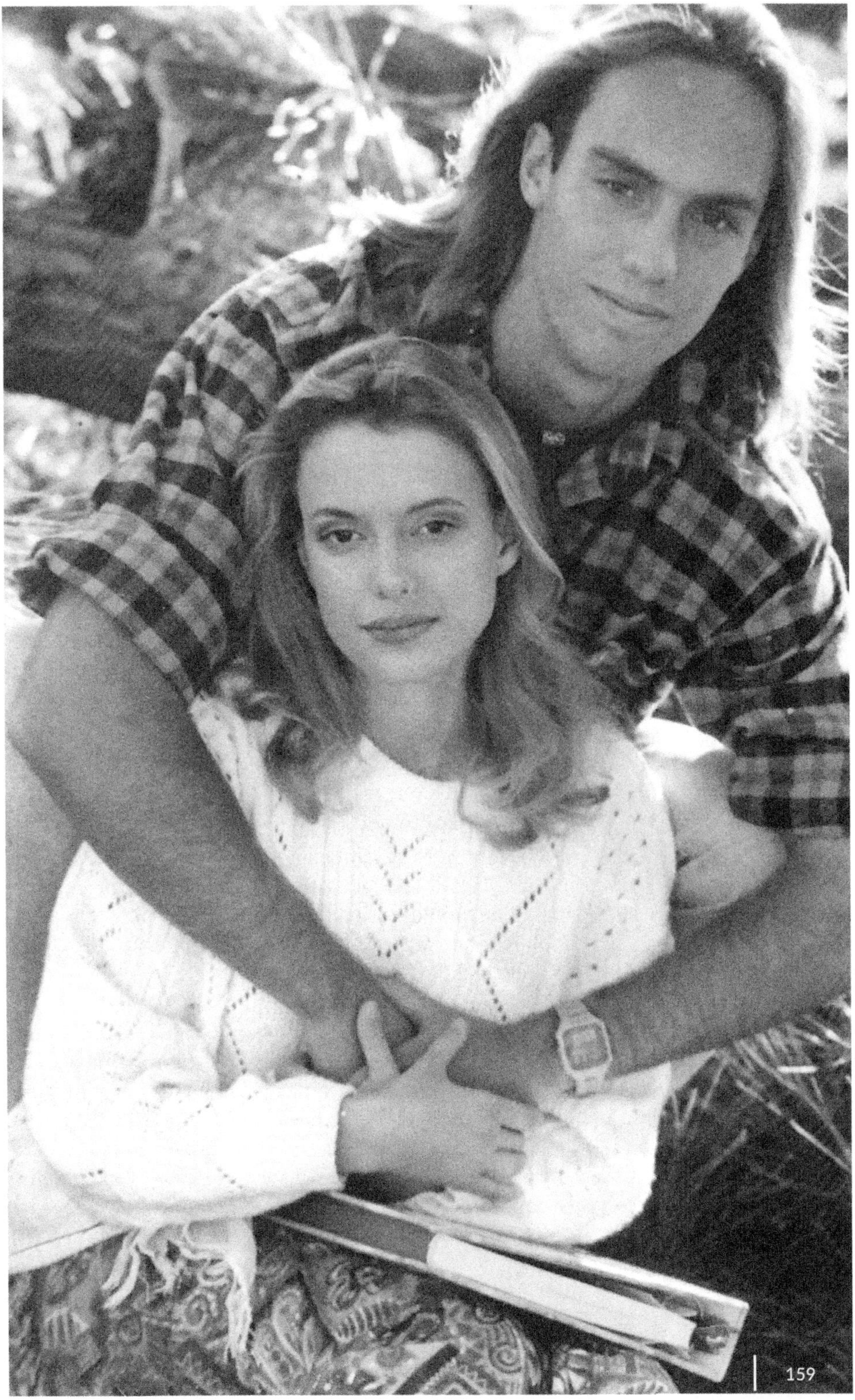

healthcare. The family relocated to Sydney, where Nick spent the week at his sales job and laboured on weekends to supplement his modest income.

In his new role, Nick quickly found success in sales and, after only two years, was headhunted by a much larger ASX-listed company. Nick climbed the career ladder in this new company and moved into a management role after five or six years. The family had also grown, and now, with three boys in tow, Nick and Melissa moved to Queensland, where Nick took up the role of State Manager. Over three years as State Manager QLD, Nick built a high-performing team through a hands-on approach, consistently hitting sales growth targets. The company, however, had a disjointed and underperforming team in Victoria. On the back of his success in Queensland, the Managing Director asked Nick if he would be interested in moving to Victoria and getting it "back on track." So, never one to back down from a challenge, Nick once again packed up his family and relocated to Melbourne.

While he was there, Nick had a chance encounter at a trade show, with a small business owner who was successfully selling healthcare products but nearing retirement. This sparked an idea, and Nick decided to purchase the company Healthcare Lifting Specialists. Despite his enthusiasm, their main obstacle was a lack of money. However, viewing this obstacle as an opportunity, Nick and Melissa set about negotiating with banks and the vendor to structure a deal where they would acquire 30% of the business and the balance in three years' time. Reflecting on this period, Nick acknowledges the risks involved but notes, "But when you remove the risk, you remove any reward."

While this happened, Melissa took on freelance administrative work for real estate agencies, which offered her the flexibility and freedom she needed. Initially, she planned to assist Nick with his new endeavour during her downtime. However, as the three-year takeover period unfolded, Melissa found herself fully immersed, steering the ship around the clock.

Nick sees Melissa as his "superpower." After nearly thirty years side by side, he notes that they "complement each other well in so many ways." They understand that their relationship, shared history, and deep mutual respect make them a formidable team in business. Nick firmly believes that "together, they can achieve so much more than either could on their own."

It wasn't all plain sailing; having bought the company in 2007 and still owing money to the vendor and the banks, the global financial crash hit in 2008. They were buying their products from Europe and also had to deal with the declining Australian dollar at that time. It meant that their prices needed to be adjusted immediately, ensuring that they hedged on the effects of the crash, as well as the fluctuations in foreign exchange. He says, "It was a steep learning curve, and we had to adjust quickly." It was "an opportunity and a challenge," but things improved, and the exchange rate returned to its normal level as the world recovered.

"The bigger business gets, the bigger the problems get."

Acquiring Healthcare Lifting Specialists took a lot of work. They entered into a contract that allowed them to purchase the business over three years, with a final payment of 70% of the total due in 2010. When the time came, they managed to reduce some of the debt but couldn't raise enough funds to cover the remainder. To bridge the gap, they brought in investors, ultimately securing 65% ownership of the business for themselves. Today, they fully own the company, but they view that challenging period positively. It was not only a time of finding investors but also a period during which they encountered "three people who played a crucial role in guiding [them] through those early days of business."

Seventeen years later, the business has grown to specialise in healthcare, focusing on improving people's quality of life. Now known as HLS, the company provides equipment solutions that enhance the lives of the elderly and disabled. They source the latest assistive technology from around the world and bring it to Australia to help providers implement these innovations for better clinical outcomes and greater corporate efficiency.

Nick asserts that a significant portion of the population includes consumers with disabilities, and smart businesses recognise this: "Acknowledging this and designing processes and physical environments to cater to this segment is not just a social responsibility but also a commercial opportunity." He adds, "We view ourselves as consultants who design equipment, solutions, and environments that promote inclusivity and social responsibility while also capitalising on the commercial potential of these consumers in the marketplace."

To illustrate the impact of Nick and Melissa's company, they share the story of an eight-year-old girl born with disabilities who required full-time care. His company was provided the opportunity to conduct a comprehensive review of how they could enhance the quality of life for both the girl and her parents, who were her primary caregivers. Nick recalls, "We went into their home and designed an equipment solution that truly changed their lives. The very next day, we received a call from her father, who was in tears, saying, 'For the first time in my little girl's life, I was able to take her to the other end of her room, open the cupboard, and let her point to what she wanted to wear for the day.'"

Another example underscores the philanthropic philosophy that drives the company. The wife of an elderly man, who had become non-verbal while in an aged care facility, approached Nick and Melissa with a heartbreaking concern. She had noticed bruising on her husband and wanted to bring him home but felt unable to care for him properly without the right equipment, yet was unable to afford it. HLS provided the necessary equipment, enabling the couple to live together at home until her husband passed away in her arms. This act of charity, initiated by the associate who visited their home, who even offered to pay for the equipment out of his own pocket, made it possible for the elderly man to return home. Without this compassionate gesture, he would not have had the chance to spend his final days in the comfort of his own home with his wife.

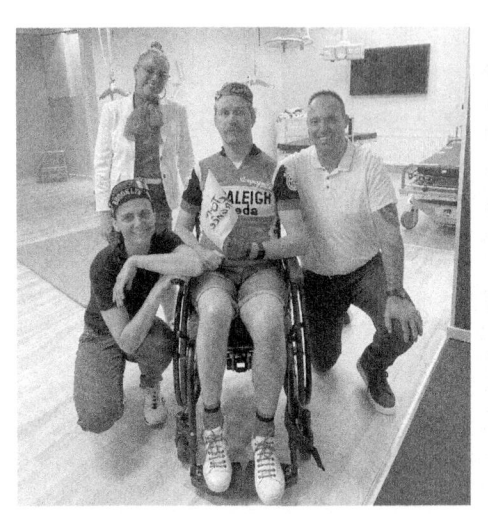

Nick reflects, "Finding the right solution takes empathy and passion. We don't see these situations as just another sales opportunity but as an opportunity to solve a problem and make a real difference in people's lives." Melissa adds, "We're harnessing an attitude of kindness and offering dignity and care. The enrichment that comes from serving others on a human level is, to me, the most meaningful purpose one can have on this earth."

For Melissa, every team member, whether a technician, installation administrator, or manager, plays a crucial role in the business and in delivering that level of care and value to customers and consumers. Perhaps due to her background, Melissa places little emphasis on CVs or prior experience. What matters more to her is a person's willingness to learn, their ability to develop skills, and most importantly, their capacity for empathy and genuine care.

Nick and Melissa have an in-depth understanding of their clientele and how they may often be overlooked or "not listened to." With this in mind, they ensure their colleagues on the front line always listen intently to what is being said. Nick is proudest when he sees his business's positive impact on people and his employees achieving success in the company. He states, "When we take somebody on and teach them about our industry, our products, and how we do things, then they start to thrive because we've got the culture fit right and they align with our values; I get massive satisfaction."

They recognise the geographical challenges posed by such a vast country, particularly since most of their products are individually designed and cannot be purchased online. Nick refers to this as "the tyranny of distance," especially when their products require professional installation. To overcome this hurdle, they are exploring acquisitions of established businesses in key regions, allowing them to extend their reach and service capabilities more effectively.

Nick and Melissa envision their next growth phase in two key ways: "One is organic growth through geographical expansion, capitalising on emerging opportunities. The other is growth through strategic acquisitions." Their long-term vision is to transform the current $10 million business into an $80 million enterprise with a strong presence nationwide. They aim to continue being the leading supplier in their field within Australia's healthcare industry. Apart from their stunning business success, the pair also have an incredible personal relationship. Nick admits, "The odds were against us, and there is no secret to a successful marriage—it's bloody hard work!" There may not be one thing that makes a long and happy marriage, but for Nick and Melissa, "not giving up" has probably allowed them to ride the wave and stick together through thick and thin. After three boys, their marriage hasn't wavered, and Melissa admits her heart still flutters when she sees Nick's car coming up the driveway. It's a testament to their love, passion, and friendship that they can work well together in both business and life.

"Humility is an important part of not questioning yourself but questioning your knowledge."

"Most of us in this world don't really know what we're doing. But the ones that achieve success are the ones that don't let it be a barrier."

HOW TO SURVIVE AND THRIVE

VOLUME II

CRISTIAN CAPONI
Property Investor

Cristian Caponi

A t just nineteen years old, Cristian stands out as the youngest contributor to the Survive and Thrive series, bringing a fresh perspective that is both inspiring and insightful. Though there is a seventy-year age gap between us, Cristian embodies qualities that resonate deeply with me. His passion for his work, relentless drive, and sheer determination to carve out his own path are traits that transcend age and experience. It's clear that Cristian possesses the spirit of a true entrepreneur—someone who is not just dreaming about success but actively pursuing it with a vigour and commitment that is rare at any age.

Cristian was born and raised in Australia to Italian parents, an upbringing that allowed him to enjoy the best of both worlds. Throughout his formative years, he frequently travelled between the two countries, fostering a deep connection with Italy that would shape his future aspirations. Reflecting on this experience, he shares, "Seeing the Italian lifestyle at a young age set the stage for me. I knew from then on that when I grew older, Italy was where I wanted to be." This dual-cultural upbringing provided Cristian with a unique perspective, blending the laid-back, family-oriented ethos of Italy with the ambitious, opportunity-driven mindset of Australia. This blend would later influence his approach to business, where he would merge the importance of work-life balance with a relentless pursuit of success.

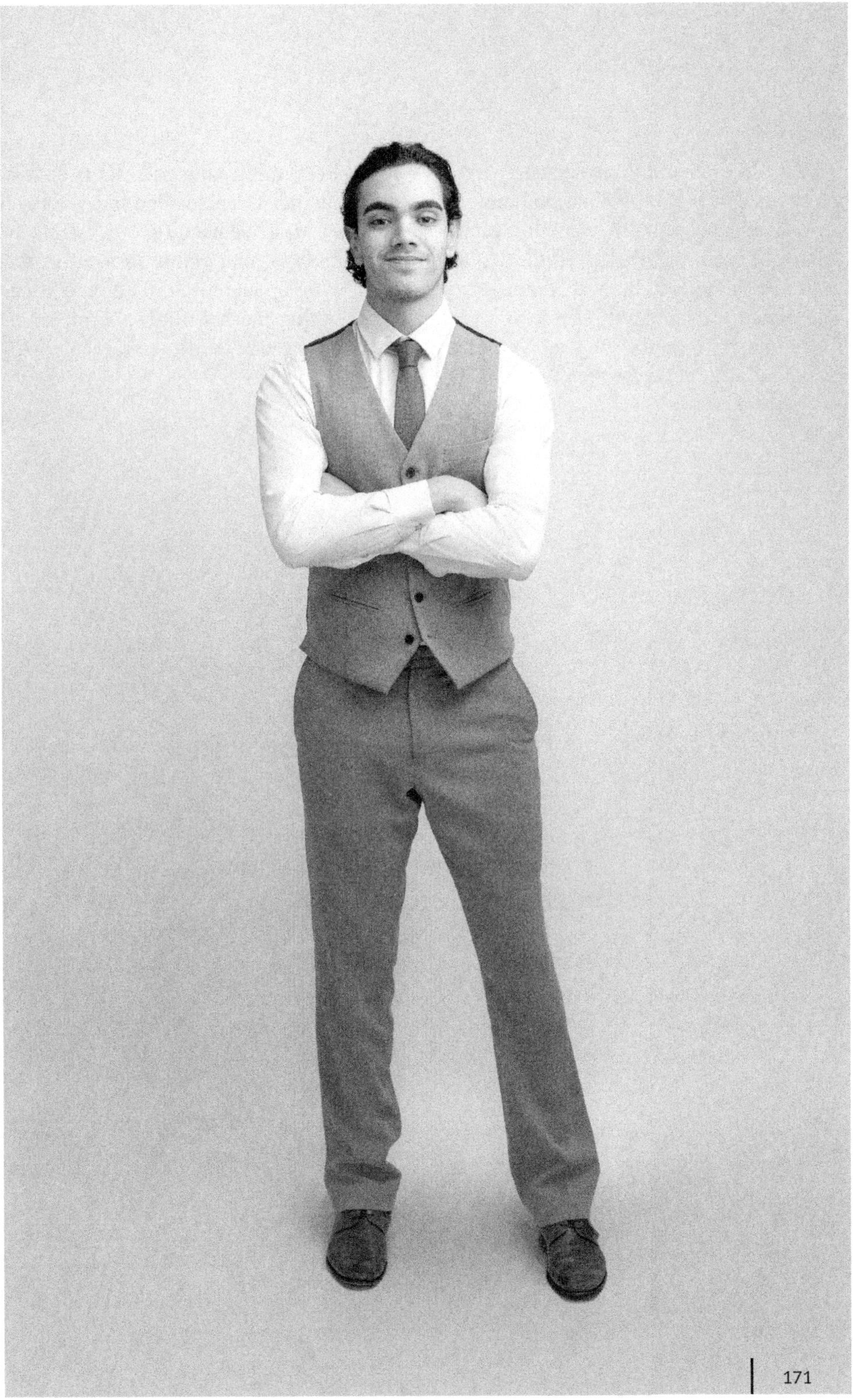

Whilst Cristian didn't particularly enjoy school, everything changed when he was given a school laptop. What had once been disengagement transformed into a hunger for learning, though not in the traditional sense. Instead of focusing on the lessons the school offered, Cristian used the laptop to his advantage, immersing himself in real estate. As he puts it, he was "on property 24/7," staying up late into the night to attend seminars and webinars, researching real estate, studying market trends, and learning from industry experts. He was particularly drawn to property investment, recognising its potential to generate wealth and provide financial security.

> "Challenges are where you find out who you really are."

After finishing school with a clear vision of a future in property, Cristian secured his first job in real estate. Though he gained valuable insights into the market, he quickly realised that a modest salary of 30,000 Australian dollars wasn't substantial enough to allow him to purchase his first property. So, just weeks before his eighteenth birthday, he made the bold decision to leave his job and join a property investment agency to gain hands-on experience in real estate investing and learn from the best in the industry.

During this time, Cristian quickly realised the importance of networking and building relationships within the industry. He understood that success in real estate was not just about what you know but also about who you know. Cristian also began to develop his own investment strategies, learning how to analyse market trends, identify emerging opportunities, and make data-driven decisions. This hands-on experience allowed Cristian to refine his approach to real estate investing and build a solid foundation for his future success.

For Cristian, following this path also meant skipping university, and his parents, who had always emphasised the importance of education, were understandably concerned about the potential risks of his decision. However, just two months after his eighteenth birthday, Cristian was able to purchase his first property, which he then refinanced in order to acquire a second property.

Cristian states that skipping university was not about rejecting education but about choosing a different form of learning. He believed that real-world experience and hands-on learning were just as valuable, if not more so, than a formal education. His decision to dive headfirst into the world of real estate allowed him to gain practical experience and build a portfolio of properties at a young age, setting him on a path to financial independence. And, after observing his drive and passion, Cristian's parents came around to his decision and began supporting his unconventional journey toward success.

Nevertheless, this path wasn't always an easy one, and Cristian still vividly remembers the insecurity he felt when he decided to leave the security of his job. As he explains, "I was overwhelmed, facing so many challenges and variables in property investment. It all hit me at once." Without a mentor or anyone to turn to for guidance, Cristian felt isolated, "just trying to learn, learn, learn." In retrospect, he realises that one of his most important lessons was understanding the value of seeking support, talking to others, and learning from their experiences. Reflecting on that challenging period, he acknowledges how his tendency to overthink and be "super analytical" trapped him in a cycle of negativity.

Cristian's struggles during this time were not just about the challenges of property investment but also about the emotional toll of navigating these challenges alone. The pressure of making the right decisions, combined with the fear of failure, created a sense of isolation and self-doubt. Cristian's analytical nature, which had served him well in his research and decision-making, now became a double-edged sword as he found himself trapped in a cycle of overthinking and second-guessing his choices.

During this difficult period, Cristian learned the importance of resilience and perseverance. He realised that setbacks and challenges were a natural part of the journey to success and that the key to overcoming them was to keep moving forward, even when the path was unclear. He began to adopt a more balanced approach to decision-making, learning to trust his instincts and take calculated risks without letting fear and doubt hold him back.

Cristian also learned the value of seeking support and guidance from others. He realised that he didn't have to navigate the challenges of property investment on his own and that there were others who had gone through similar experiences and could offer valuable advice. Cristian began to reach out to mentors and experienced investors, seeking their insights and learning from their mistakes. This willingness to seek help and learn from others became a turning point in Cristian's journey, allowing him to overcome his challenges and move forward with renewed confidence.

As a young man (not yet twenty years old), Cristian faced significant challenges securing financing and had to navigate the process the hard way. He explains, "At seventeen, I worked for a year and saved as much as I could." To build his credit score, he began using a credit card for purchases and made sure to pay off the balance immediately. Cristian's commitment to saving and financial discipline allowed him to accumulate the funds needed for his first property purchase at a young age.

Cristian initially explored various affordable areas across Australia before focusing on Perth. After analysing market trends, he observed a promising upswing in the Perth property market. Although the data looked encouraging, the fact that he was based in Sydney and would be investing without physically viewing the property, which was more than two thousand miles away, made him hesitant. Despite these challenges, Cristian took the leap. Reflecting on his decision, he remarks, "It has turned out to be one of the best areas to purchase an investment property in the past twelve months."

This experience taught Cristian the importance of location in real estate. He knew that even if the property required extensive renovations, its location in a high-demand area would ultimately drive its value up, making it a sound investment. Cristian's approach to real estate investing was based

"If you think negative,
you'll end up being negative."

on a long-term perspective, where he focused on properties that had the potential to appreciate in value over time rather than seeking quick profits.

Cristian's advice for other budding property investors in Australia is to either "buy one expensive property or buy cheaper properties and get more of them," a strategy that reflects his belief in the importance of diversification and risk management in real estate investing. By spreading his investments across multiple properties, Cristian can mitigate the risks associated with market fluctuations and ensure a steady stream of income from his rental properties.

Cristian's approach to diversification is rooted in his understanding of risk management. He knows that relying on a single property or a single market can be risky, as market conditions can change unexpectedly. By diversifying his portfolio, Cristian is able to spread his risk and protect his investments from potential downturns in any one market. In addition to diversification, Cristian also emphasises the importance of conducting thorough research and due diligence before making any investment decisions. He believes that informed decision-making is key to successful investing and that investors should always be prepared for the unexpected. Cristian's meticulous approach to research and analysis has allowed him to make sound investment decisions and build a successful real estate portfolio at a young age.

Cristian's long-term vision is a key factor in his success. He understands that building wealth and achieving financial independence is a marathon not a sprint. Cristian is patient and disciplined in his approach, recognising that the rewards of real estate investing come over time as properties appreciate in value and generate rental income. This long-term perspective allows Cristian to stay focused on his goals, even in the face of challenges and setbacks.

With a substantial portfolio established in Australia, Cristian is now looking to invest in America, aiming to add "a little bit more fun" to his ventures. At just nineteen, he envisions owning property in Italy before he turns thirty, driven by his ambitious goals and forward-thinking approach. Remarkably, Cristian is not motivated by fast cars or sharp suits; instead, he has a deep passion for helping others. Family is important, and, after observing how hard both his parents have worked, another short-term goal he has in mind is being able to pay off their mortgage. He also aspires to open a school for underprivileged boys, believing, as he puts it, "When I'm on my deathbed, I won't remember the cars, but I will remember helping others and leaving a legacy."

Cristian's journey is far from over. At just nineteen years old, he has already achieved remarkable success, but he is not content to rest on his laurels. He is constantly looking ahead, setting new goals, and pushing himself to achieve even greater heights. His vision for the future is clear: he wants to continue building his real estate portfolio, invest in new markets, and use his wealth and knowledge to make a positive impact on the world.

"Reverse engineer your goals."

HOW TO SURVIVE AND THRIVE

VOLUME II

JOHN ATTRIDGE

Founder and CEO of BBXUK,
Keynote Speaker and Author

John Attridge

I remember, back in the day, way before I founded Reebok, my first wage packet for a week's work was eleven pounds and five shillings. So when John recounted his journey from growing up on a farm and earning money as a farmhand at just nine years old, it reminded me of a bygone era when money was never just given out, it had to be earned. Born in Australia, and now based in Bournemouth, John is a keynote speaker, author, and umpire for the England and Wales Cricket Board.

Growing up on a dairy farm in Australia, John became accustomed to working hard for a living. Tending to 140 acres of land with about seventy cows that needed milking twice a day, every day of the week, and every week of the year, farm life instilled a strong work ethic in the young boy. And, by the time he was nine years old, he was earning "five cents an hour, slashing bracken fern, feeding the young cows, and helping clean out the cow yard."

"It's not what you know, it's who you know, and who they know, that becomes very useful."

In addition to all the physical hard work, John was catching a 7 a.m. school bus and then arriving home at 5 p.m. to do his chores, which included "feeding the ferrets, and the dogs and putting on the dinner." He explains how different life was back then, "It was a hard life before digitisation, there were no Game Boys, we had to make our own entertainment, but it certainly set the scene for later in life in terms of the value of work."

Although his home was set in acres of land, there was a sense of camaraderie with the neighbouring farmers and John fondly remembers how they'd "work with the neighbours. Everybody would muck in and cut hay, and cart it back into the shed." For him, the bonds and friendships formed through hard work and cooperation ended up being "vital lessons."

Eventually, John left the farm to study for an economics degree at La Trobe University, and he recounts an unusual scenario in which his economics tutor taught him how to invest in the stock market by taking him to the betting shop and showing him how to gamble. He remembers a project in which all undergraduates were given $10 to invest in the stock market. John purchased shares in Mr Whippy for one cent, and within the year, the share rose to forty cents a share, giving John a healthy profit, and putting him top of the class for that particular exercise. His passion for the stock market had been ignited.

"Stay calm, make calculated decisions, and think issues through to the end."

However, he soon found that he had a natural talent for the art of selling and became the "youngest superintendent in charge of a group of men at the age of twenty-one." In just a few short years, John rose in the ranks to become the Southern State Sales Manager, a position that led him to start his own car rental business with a former associate. It was the late 1980s, and the two young men "walked away with a million dollars worth of finance, without personal guarantees… and a lot of brand-new Mazda cars."

The business was based in Queensland's Gold Coast and, with the World Expo in Brisbane, timing was everything. John explains that "people were coming from all over the world to visit all the exhibitions from every country in the world, all under one roof in the Brisbane showgrounds [so] we had one hundred percent occupancy, which is almost unheard of." The rarity of full capacity lasted for "the better part of ten months." Things were looking good for the Attridge family, with money pouring into the car rental business and John's father selling his farm "for a good sum of money," which allowed him to retire in his mid-forties.

However, just a year later, the 1989 Australian pilots' strike brought everything to an abrupt halt. It was one of the most expensive industrial disputes in Australian history and affected both national and international flights, with serious knock-on effects for businesses. It was not something that John could have planned for and whilst the industrial action lasted for five months, John's business was already struggling only a few weeks into the strike. With no revenue coming in, they were still having to pay off loans, staff wages, the leasehold on properties, and other fixed overheads. John reveals that they "had gone from hero to zero in the space of a smack in the face."

Nevertheless, he approaches life with the philosophy that if he can do something about a problem, he'll take immediate, swift, and aggressive action to implement a strategy. But if he decides there is no solution, then he quips, "I go to the pub and have a beer because I never worry about something I've got no control over."

In this instance, John was agile, and he used his connections to form an organisation that was later to become "one of the largest independently owned trade exchanges." It's impressive to think that this was all done before the internet, apps, or mobile phones. Before everything was digitised, John had to physically put together a directory, which he describes as being "a little bit like the Yellow Pages." Every month, his team would put the documents together, manually place them in envelopes, address, and then post them out to each individual recipient. He recognises how "cumbersome, slow, and time-consuming" it all was but also expresses the advantage "that it encouraged face-to-face meetings... which is the most superior and most effective form of human communication."

"Have less emotion and think through the process before action."

Through sheer effort and perseverance, John was able to create a circular economy where business owners were able to work with each other within a community that started with fifty people and has now grown to nearly half a million. The premise was based on the concept of "spare capacity." John explains that "it's the ability to take on more customers, sell more stuff, do more, and gain more revenue without increasing fixed costs." He suggests every business has spare capacity; it's a formula that requires businesses to measure the spare capacity and then do something with it. Selling the spare capacity increases revenue, but in line with John's business model, using digital trade credits, instead of money, can offset existing cash costs in order to protect cash flow.

As a best-selling author and keynote speaker on how to start, grow, scale, and exit, John has some invaluable lessons on how to deal with adversity. He suggests that "a fool can spend a lot of money when they're making a lot of money and be able to cruise along. But it's when you know every penny counts that you've got to analyse the situation, see the bigger picture, and work out what you could do to solve the problem that faces you."

To ensure that your business is sustainable, John advises having more than just one form of revenue. He believes there are many business owners who rarely think of developing recurring and multiple revenue streams. His most recent venture, BBX, has had four streams of revenue from day one. He set up a performance revenue and supplementary revenue, explaining that "if one dries up, you can still work with the other."

The business model of BBX is explained with a case study focusing on an individual who organises and curates specialised events for high-net-worth people. She buys tickets at good wholesale rates from the venues then resells them with a mark-up. Occasionally, she may get stuck with leftover tickets, and therefore has spare capacity that will eat into her profits. On one occasion as a BBX community member, she was able to sell her leftover tickets, earning digital trade credits. The process is quick and agile, and John claims, "If the Titanic had been a bit more nimble and agile, it wouldn't have hit the iceberg, and that could be the way in business."

The digital credits earned were then used to purchase a stand at the 'meetings show' for a reduced rate. Being able to attend this show in London, which would normally have been unaffordable, enabled the event organiser to meet a client who became her highest earner, turning her spare capacity into her highest profit.

"Cash flow is like a river. You've either gotta make it rain upstream or build a bigger dam to stop it escaping downstream."

John claims that as the business grew, the concept of using digital trade credits was seen to be challenging "government, banks and the big end of town," and they were no longer able to "operate under the radar." He explains how "someone approached the Australian government and said that we were operating illegally." The business operations were purportedly against the prescribed interest section of the Corporations Act and he received a letter from the government, informing him that the company had to comply with the agreed industry operational procedures (IOPs), or cease trading.

After five years of business with several thousand customers, this was a major setback. To combat the threat, the International Reciprocal Trade Association, Australasian Division, was formed and was able to "convince the government that the IOPs that they had signed off on were impractical." After about six months, the government produced an amended IOPs that would work for the industry as a whole. Thankfully for John, this meant that the digital trade credit at the heart of the business model became a legitimate currency.

For John, there's no greater satisfaction than when a client realises his platform has rescued their business. By using a wide range of technologies to connect people, and maintain a circular economy, he demonstrates how being part of his business community can transform companies through better cash flow, increasing profits, helping growth, and selling for larger profits. He relays a case study of an individual who had a lighting business with "50 grand's worth of stock that was gathering dust." Joining the community allowed the individual to sell off $48,000 worth of stock using digital trade credits. He then sold the company a few months later, "as a direct result of those extra sales that would have been written off stock." Due to the sale of his stock, he was able to increase the turnover amount by $48,000, which increased the sale price by $96,000. Selling his lighting business for $400,000 was a joy for John to hear, who was pivotal in increasing the individual's sale price by 25%.

John has countless examples of how, in growing his own business, he was able to contribute to the success of other enterprises, benefiting both newcomers and well-established companies. One such story he shares is about a "rising entrepreneur" who had an excess stock of towel sets he was selling door to door. According to John, they were ordered by the Sheraton Hotel in Fiji but were the incorrect weight, so became obsolete. John offered him a place at the regular expos he would organise, where members of the community could buy and sell goods using the digital trade credits. The first half of the towel stock took three months to sell door-to-door, whereas the other half, through the expo, only took a few hours to completely sell out.

With so much valuable information and strategic insight to share, John wrote a book titled *Business Blunders and Bloody Great Ideas* to help others achieve in business. His book features a piece of advice from Stephen R. Covey to entrepreneurs, which is to "start with the end in mind." And John admits that, if he knew this when he started, he "would have been far better off," suggesting that people tend to plan their holidays in more detail than they do their business. His book also leans on the Pareto Principle, which suggests that 80% of outcomes come from 20% of causes. Measuring and monitoring spare capacity is also, not surprisingly, a fixture within John's book, "because it's the biggest hidden asset, despite every business being blissfully unaware of it."

"Be civil to people and tolerate fools. Whatever you want to look like in the mirror, ensure that the people you associate with look like that too."

HOW TO
SURVIVE
AND
THRIVE
VOLUME II

Let's share wisdom!

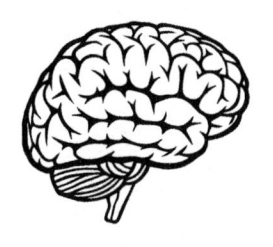

"When you want to improve, remember IDEO; integrate, delegate, eliminate, and outsource."

Jen Goldman
Business Transformer

"To unlock efficiency and automation, don't be afraid to build new things."

JJ Englert
Community and Education Lead at Softr

"No matter what business you're in, look to the service industry and see how the best do it. Great customer service is the key, so be the bartender that throws the cocktail napkin down and says, 'I will be right with you.'"

John Sneider
Founder and CEO of Wild Gravity

"It's better to lead a great life
than to go after greatness."

Joe Chatham
Founder of USA 500 Clubs LLC

"If you have hope, you have everything you need;
if you share that, you'll have a rush of hope."

John Adamcik
Director of Human Resources

"Don't allow fear to control your life.
Instead, figure out what you fear and
go out and crush it."

Kara Goldin
Former CEO of Hint Water

"Stay present, engaged, and connected
to yourself and those around you."

Juliet Bellagambi
Founder of PetalTalks

"You can only control two things in your life: how you react and what steps you take next. Everything else is out of your control, so just let it go."

Kat Jovey
Customer Success Enablement Specialist at Enable

"Harness the power of positivity. A positive environment can enhance productivity and build creativity. A few words of encouragement or a little moment of kindness can really transform our workplace."

Kim Bennett
Author

"Living longer has a lot to do with where we live. Create an environment where healthy choices are made easier."

Kas Bordier
Longevity Entrepreneur & Investor

"Shift back into the driver's seat and take control of your mental, physical, emotional, and spiritual health. From there, everything will fall into place."

Kim Prince
Founder and CSO of KOIN Systems

"When people come to you with a problem, they're probably not asking for your advice. Instead, ask questions. The self-reflection will start to set in and the solution will become clear."

Laura King
Executive Leadership Coach

"The more you listen, the more prepared you are to speak."

Lisa Bowman
Founder of Marketing Mojo

"Finding those windows for yourself where you can have unfocused productivity will drive you to success."

Lavni Varyani
Founding Partner of Pharma BP

"No matter how successful you've been in life, we all need help and support to reach our goals. Asking for help is not a weakness. It is a strength."

Laura Vann LaRusso
Communication Skills Coach

"If you're a leader, you have to stay connected with others."

Lee Ellis
Leadership Coach and Author

"Being human-centred will provide value to your customers, support for your employees, and mental well-being for you."

Lis Hubert
Founding Partner of CX by Design

"Don't be afraid to believe in yourself and your ideas, even when others don't share your vision because you may be trailblazing. True innovators use unconventional methods, so when nothing exists to accommodate your innovation, forge a new path."

Lori D. Coombs
Earthdate Infrastructure Systems at NASA

"Think about the simplest and easiest way you can go about a task. If it seems overwhelming, start with the most simple and manageable step, do it, and then move on to the next step."

Maggie Perotin
Business and Leadership Coach

"Develop yourself spiritually."

Mark Dawes
Executive Coach

"Embrace the power of imperfection. If you can find a way to embrace what you think may be painful or ugly, it may be your road to sharing your gift with the world."

Lourdes Gant
Co-owner of Manatee Holdings Ltd.

"What would you do if money was no object? What do you waste time on? Follow that. Because the answer to your happiness and success comes from what lights you up, not what is going to make other people happy."

Lori Hamilton
Founder and President of Prosperity Productions

"Experiment, and that's how you will start your journey with productivity."

Manish Bhardia
CEO of Aimey.ai

"Life is like a book, made up of many chapters. Never be afraid to open a new chapter in your book, it will lead to personal growth and new life experiences."

Lisa Roads
Founder of The Holiday Property Coach

"Your number one cost in life is going to be taxes. Most other things are an investment. So engage with a tax strategist or a legal advisor to change the trajectory of your business."

Mark J. Kohler
Senior Partner at KKOS Lawyers, LLP

"We are capable of reinventing ourselves every day. Make your life better."

Mark Mills
Business Leader and Investor

"You are blessed with 86,400 seconds each day. Do you invest them in your happiness and growth or do you waste them? Use this as your compass."

Maher Kaddoura
Management Consultant and Serial Entrepreneur

"If you're dreading going in to work, refocus your purpose, find something that brings you joy and use it to earn a living."

Mark W. Lamplugh
CEO of South Jersey Treatment Management Company

"There are risks and costs to action, but they are far less than the risks of comfortable inaction."

Maureen Hammett
Leadership Coach

"Take a step back and believe that people are putting in the effort, despite appearances. Give them the time to prove themselves."

Matt Whitmore
Managing Partner at BWC Real Estate

GAYATREE DIPCHAN

Psychologist, Behaviour Change Consultant,
NLP Practitioner and Facilitator

Gayatree Dipchan

D uring my interviews with the remarkable contributors of *How to Survive and Thrive*, I am usually left awed by the inner strength and determination that they display, alongside an ability to change their trajectory and manoeuvre themselves into a better place swiftly and fearlessly. Many of the stories in this book focus on professional journeys or financial affairs, but occasionally, there are true life and death survival stories, and this particular one from Gayatree was quite affecting in its brutality. At a time in her life when she should have been riding the wave of success, something unthinkable happened to Gayatree, which propelled her into a dismal state of pain, anguish, and eventual healing.

"Be clear with your intentions and expectations. Trust and reliability are not built on what is said but on the consistency of what is done."

Born in Trinidad, Gayatree spent most of her childhood in the southern islands of the Caribbean, during the oil and gas boom. Her great-grandparents were indentured labourers brought in from India during the colonial period. Before oil and gas were discovered during her grandparents' tenure, her family was working in sugar and rice fields and coffee and cocoa plantations, so this boom allowed her grandparents and parents to thrive financially and provide their children with better educational opportunities. She describes growing up in a "very traditional Indian home, with a very large extended family" where everyone lived and worked as a community. However, within this, also remained the societal norms of generations before her, in which alcohol and abuse were expected coping mechanisms for hardship.

Gayatree describes her father as highly intelligent despite only being educated up to primary school level. Like many others who possessed the skills to learn but not the opportunity, he viewed formal education as a necessity and did everything in his power to ensure that his own children had the benefit of the education he missed out on. He made sure that they were all educated to degree level, "paying for everything from

"Healing from trauma isn't about therapy and living one day at a time. It is a journey of reflection, mourning who you used to be, and relearning how to live life from a different lens, one filled with self-compassion, loyalty to your own beliefs, and an empowering self-love."

accommodation to anything [they] wanted to do." She saw her father as a person who always supported his children and encouraged them to achieve more than he could in his lifetime. He faced personal challenges that impacted her relationship with him growing up, but in adulthood, Gayatree's understanding that it was his childhood experiences that shaped his behaviours and choices has led to forgiveness and grace in their relationship during his later years.

At the age of twenty, Gayatree had the opportunity to move to the UK on a "working holiday programme." Although she had studied for a degree in business before moving, she felt that it didn't challenge her or give her an inner sense of achievement. While at the time, her family saw her goals as unreasonable, she craved a more people-centric career that could facilitate change in some way. So she pivoted and undertook a master's degree in psychology and then a further master's degree in human rights law. Gayatree explains, "I like working with people, I prefer human behaviour, understanding why people do what they do."

It was while studying in London that Gayatree met her husband-to-be, a Trinidadian who had come over to the UK to study for a master's at Imperial College through a scholarship scheme. Mark was already working for a UK oil and gas company with assets in the Caribbean. So, by the time Gayatree was twenty-eight years old, with two master's degrees under her belt, several years of trauma-focused clinical supervision in psychology, and aspirations to continue her academic research, she found herself back in the Caribbean, with expectations of returning to the UK with her future husband, where she could continue with her career with his support.

For Gayatree, returning to her homeland was extremely challenging, as she had fallen in love with life in Britain and the dreams she had for her future. She explains that on her return to Trinidad, "I had no friends... and was quite lonely." Everyone in her circle had moved on to adventures that were very different from her own. Her isolation was exacerbated by her inability to find a job within the field she had spent so many years studying for. However, there seemed to be a light at the end of the tunnel when Mark introduced her to Latoya Shand, a psychologist he had studied with back in Jamaica. Latoya introduced her to a small but progressive firm where she also worked, and things finally started to move in the direction she had hoped for.

It was at the time Gayatree began to feel a shift in herself, a sense of belonging with a group of people who recognised her skills and complemented her practice as a psychologist. In this space, she found a group of friends who have remained a part of her journey to this day. Life, however, has a wonderful way of throwing you curveballs when you least expect it. One early morning a month after starting in her new job, an assailant pushed his way into her office and sexually assaulted her, causing grievous bodily harm to the extent that she needed facial reconstructive surgery.

Although the events of that day will no doubt have left an indelible stain on her psyche, it was the spiritual intermission she experienced during the attack that has remained vivid. Gayatree was brought up with the Hindu faith and still lives life in the path of Hinduism. As she was being punched in the face and strangled, unable to breathe, she turned within and called out, 'Shiva.' She recalled a memory of her childhood where her father's godfather, a gentle giant, told her about Shiva and how he would answer all prayers. Taking a philosophical approach, Gayatree describes "Shiva [as] the destroyer of what holds you back within yourself."

As a five-foot-three-inch woman up against a six-foot aggressor, Gayatree went within, to that place of 'knowing.' She explains how she "just said 'Shiva,' and to the right, behind the man's shoulder, was a vision of a beautiful man, and it was Shiva." She was left with fifteen fractures to her face, permanent hearing loss, and further fractures along her ribs. She had also been thrown to the floor and sexually assaulted. The heinous ordeal must have seemed like it would never end, but throughout it, Gayatree claims to have had no sensation in her lower body, "feeling absolutely nothing." She also attributes her survival to her inner state at the time of the attack: "I was sitting cross-legged in the centre and Shiva was over me with a smile, not as a physical body but as an energy. I was happy, sitting in that vortex, and I remember thinking that I didn't want to leave... the only way I can describe it, is to say it was bliss."

There are plenty of anecdotes and professional insights that can both substantiate and question Gayatree's experience, and she is aware that most people would struggle to understand the reality of her vision. Regardless of whether it was divine intervention or something psychological that kicked in at a time of extreme terror, for Gayatree, it was Shiva who helped her not only survive but indeed thrive in her refusal to be defined by this one day in her life.

After the assailant fled, Gayatree was discovered by Latoya, who became her lifeline and best friend. She spent the next five days in hospital under constant monitoring due to brain swelling and uncertainty about her regaining the use of her eyes. One year later, she underwent reconstructive surgery on the left side of her face, to replace the shattered bones with metal plates. While her physical injuries were slowly healing, she was facing emotional turmoil because of her own inability to understand and share what had happened to her, due to the social stigma around sexual assault against women. Gayatree's primary support came from her mother, sister, and cousin, Elizabeth. In her wider community, sexual violence was seen as something to be whispered about but never openly shared or discussed, perpetuating feelings of shame and self-blame. Even today, working within the same communities, Gayatree notes that the rape and assault of young girls is still met with gossip and social alienation rather than compassion and the opportunity to give a voice to their experiences. She says, "You want somebody to hear your experience because you want a level of validation that you weren't wrong, it wasn't your fault."

It was a life-changing experience of the worst kind, and she didn't feel able to discuss it with friends or family. Even her fiancé, who was of a different religious faith from her, couldn't understand her experience, and she felt dismissed regarding her spiritual experience with Shiva. She explains how painful it was to keep everything inside, without anyone willing to actively and only listen. Further to this, the need to go back to the UK returned as she felt there would be more acceptance and less judgement there. Ironically for her, Gayatree's training in the UK specialised in sexual trauma, so the different societal responses to sexual trauma in the Caribbean and the UK, the different ways in which different social perceptions shape our self-concept were not lost on her.

"Every few months, pause to reflect. Visualise a timeline of three to six months, and walk through your moments, the highs and lows, the successes and challenges, and within those experiences, you will see learnings and strengths that will empower you in your present."

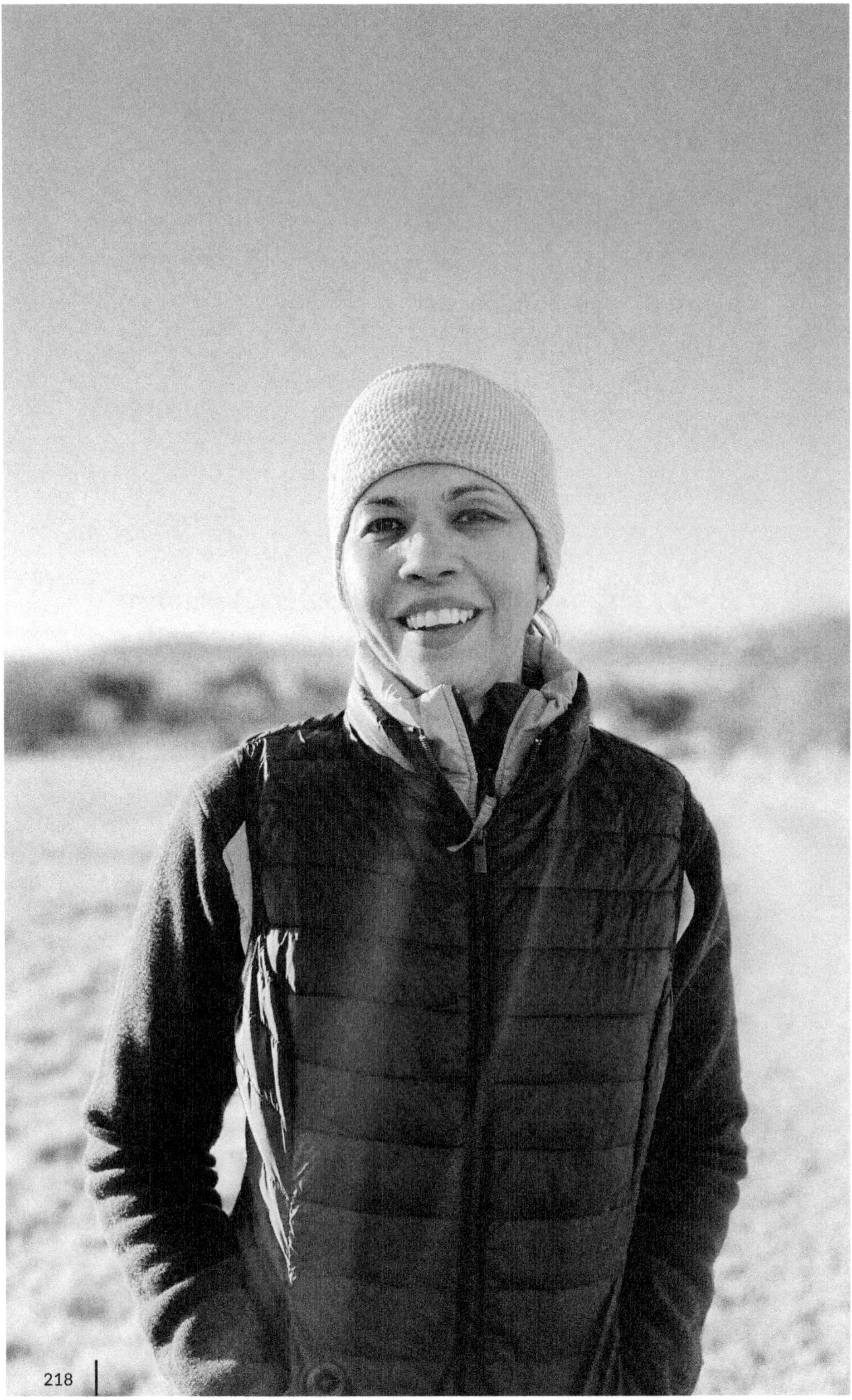

As a result of her trauma, her relationships with friends, family, and her new husband became more strained over time. In her marriage, perceived obligations and pressures from her husband's family meant she began to feel alienated and alone in her marriage. The lack of integration was particularly hard on Gayatree, who felt she was left to cope with her sexual and physical trauma alone.

In the two months after the assault, she constantly thought of suicide and ways in which she could end the emotional pain that she wasn't able to safely deal with. The relationships she had formed with Latoya became her lifeline and the anchor she didn't know she needed. Latoya was the one who found Gayatree bleeding and broken on the floor, and she became the person who, regardless of how busy life got, spoke to her every day, cried with her when she needed that open vulnerability, and cursed the world and its unfairness when it became too much. At that point, she was the only person who made certain that Gayatree felt "heard and validated."

Having specialised in sexual trauma, Gayatree is conscious that she also experienced it firsthand. She suggests that "everything I knew in theory from doing my master's programme and being in practice became irrelevant in my own experience because I could not figure out how these theories could in any way support or help me get through it." Nevertheless, she went from psychologist to psychologist before finding the help she was searching for in a person-centred practitioner who provided the gentle nurturing needed to share and process her experiences. She describes it as "getting to a very human point of view, knowing the theory behind it, but not using it in a way that the client feels that they are being clinically assessed and diagnosed. I needed that in my own healing, and that's how I practise."

Gayatree's interest in working with charities and NGOs is because of her focus on human rather than "clinical" methods. Early on, her choice was to focus on sexual trauma, and it is a testament to her resilience that, despite advice to the contrary, she continues to work in that field. Ironically, she was told that "it would be unhealthy for me and unhealthy for the client." Yet, everything inside Gayatree was telling her that her experiences made her differently qualified to "empathise" with victims and survivors of trauma.

Over the last fifteen years, Gayatree's own practice as a psychologist has evolved in response to her experiences as a patient in therapy. In her work with different cultures and populations, she feels there is a need for dynamic learning, as clients all have different ways of processing their traumatic experiences. She continues to learn through engagement with other psychologists, empirical research, and certifications in various modes of practice, but what she has observed is that, in some professional circles, there is more of a focus on diagnosis and rigid alignment to therapeutic frameworks than listening to the client and being present with them. In her own journey of finding a therapist, she began to question the lack of listening by clinical psychologists. For her, methodologies and processes such as EMDR, hypnotherapy, CBT, DBT, etc.should be used with an understanding of the client's own ability to process their trauma in their own time. Gayatree tried EMDR and CBT approaches, but at the time, her trauma was still incredibly raw and she didn't feel as though she was being listened to. In fact, she recalls a time in which a psychologist had said, "exactly what my husband had said—that my encounter with Shiva was just a figment of my imagination to cope."

As a neuro-linguistic programming professional, Gayatree is an advocate for understanding individual neurological processes, modes of language, and communication, and then shifting behavioural patterns to achieve specific goals ecologically. "I think you have to do the work within yourself as well," suggests Gayatree, and it's unsurprising to learn that she constantly works on maintaining good mental health. As an advocate for open communication, she states that she "truly believes in finding your circle and choosing wisely who you are sharing your experiences with."

Her formal training has taught her how to manage her emotional responses and to detach herself from identifying with her clients' experiences. Bringing her own spiritual practice to her learnings has informed her daily practice of meditation and mindfulness. There can be days where "six clients talking about rape or what they have been through, and helping them process their trauma" can inadvertently filter into your personal life. Switching to being a mother or wife can be difficult. However, what helps is grounding herself and practising mindfulness, "really being aware of breathing, of what you are looking at, colours, shapes, and sizes… the taste and texture

"Take a walk with the trees. Walk barefoot on the forest floor. Feel the shifting sands as the waves touch your feet. Pass your fingers through the grass. When we engage our five senses consciously, we begin to align our bodies with calmness, relaxation, and well-being."

of the food you're eating … all the sensory inputs that are happening in the moment, what you see, hear, feel, and taste."

For Gayatree, just going for peaceful walks in the forest or a nearby ocean helps. "I really focus on breathing in through my nose, filling my stomach, and breathing out through my mouth, especially when I'm outside in nature. I keep my focus on the action of breathing." She suggests that most people try to "live in the present, but their brains have a hundred different thoughts going a mile a minute." She leans on Ayurvedic knowledge to explain how "closely linked the human body is to the five elements of nature; 72% water is saliva, urine, semen, blood, and sweat; 12% earth is teeth, nails, bone, skin, and organs; 6% is responsible for all movement, contraction, vibration, expansion, and 4% fire, which forms hunger, thirst, and all other sensory reactions. The rest of it is 'ether,' which she considers to be energy.

Gayatree also suggests that regularly being in the forests and the ocean creates a space where there is natural alignment. Meditation is "active" and it's clear that she's looking for a natural balance through yoga and a connection to the earth. For many years, she worked with "very high-risk communities in Trinidad," where there was a prevalence of sexual abuse and assault of children. She has worked with young males from these communities who "would have witnessed a family member being killed through gang violence" and had a high probability of experiencing abuse ranging from neglect to child sexual assault. In her private practice, she continues working with adults who have had Adverse Childhood Experiences and intergenerational trauma.

When Gayatree decided to separate from her husband of fifteen years, "a good person who didn't know how to be a husband to me," she felt she could finally be who she needed to be. She continues with her voluntary work in the Caribbean region with NiNa Young Leaders Programme and has set up her own consultancy in Norway, collaborating with regional consultancies, such as Waypoint Limited, a change management consultancy, delivering bespoke integrative programs with engaged experiential workshops and training; and NiNa Consulting, which focuses on research and training initiatives around empowering young women in the Caribbean. She also has an online counselling and coaching practice where she continues her work in shifting narratives towards empowerment and resilience with her clients.

She is also delighted to now have her "own small temple," something she felt restricted from within her marriage. She meditates and openly enjoys the vibrations of the space. Further to this, she has shifted her own therapeutic offerings in her practice: "Everyone gets a free session, and if my energy and modalities of practice appeal to [them], they can book paying sessions." After an incredibly difficult healing process, Gayatree finally feels "that things are starting to shift... it's not bliss, but a living experience of being happy in every moment as I move forward."

Moving forward means living in Norway with her twelve-year-old daughter, and she and Mark have become friends, redefining what their family means for them. She has finally found inner peace and a feeling of safety in Stavanger, where she immerses herself in the beautiful natural environment of Scandinavia. Although she has left the Caribbean, she still keeps that part of her heritage alive through food, spiritual learnings, music, and people.

Having survived such a profound, life-changing event, demonstrating the very worst of human behaviour, Gayatree is determined not to allow someone else to take away her future. Her emotional resilience, fortitude, and strong spiritual beliefs have carried her through the despair of being alive, the struggle to stay alive, and finally re-learning what it is to find joy in living and thriving.

"Nurture your children's self-esteem with gentleness and kindness. They are small humans with big emotions trying to navigate their own understanding of their environments, their social interactions, and even their relationships with you. Practise patience and self-awareness consistently with them and how they navigate life will be reflected in their assertiveness, self-assurance, and graciousness."

HOW TO
SURVIVE
AND
THRIVE
VOLUME II

DEVON HARRIS
Olympian, Motivational Speaker, and Author

Devon Harris

At first glance, the connection between Devon, the sixty-year-old Jamaican former bobsleigher, and me might not seem obvious. Yet, we share more than one might expect. Both of us have a deep love for sports, and coincidentally, both my father and Devon were born on Christmas Day. When Devon arrived at Sandhurst in the UK for his army training, he was introduced to Reebok trainers, and he fondly recalls returning to Jamaica with them on his feet and feeling "a bit special." However, it's Devon's outlook on life where our bond truly deepens; his relentless tenacity and the belief that you must never stop and always keep pushing, no matter what, resonates with my own perspective on life and business.

Devon was born in 1964 in Kingston, Jamaica, but he was actually raised by his paternal grandmother in the rural parish of St Elizabeth. He describes the village of Haughton as "a farming community filled with mostly subsistence farmers, where people just bartered their things in the marketplace." Although there were plenty of other boys in the neighbourhood for Devon to play with, he was still too young to join them in "bird hunting and making slingshots." However, he still managed to get himself into trouble when, at just five years old, he tried to chop open a coconut with a machete and ended up with a nasty cut on his thumb instead.

Devon Harris

As the only child in the household, Devon found entertainment in his grandmother's captivating storytelling. Among the many tales she shared, the ones that left the deepest impression were about soldiers, the army, and the incredible feats they accomplished. These stories sparked Devon's young imagination, and from then on, he was determined to become a soldier when he grew up.

When it was time for Devon to start school, his father decided to bring him back to Kingston. Reflecting on this experience, Devon recalls, "I was uprooted, and it was traumatic. I had been living in the countryside, running around half-naked, having fun, and then suddenly, I had to move to Kingston to live with my dad, who I hardly knew." The contrast between the two environments was stark; he went from the wide-open freedom of rural life to "one of the inner-city areas of Kingston, where tall zinc fences separated the yards." Devon felt confined, no longer able to play freely with other children, saying, "I felt like I was in a prison."

He began school against the backdrop of Jamaica gaining its independence, a period he recalls as "...interesting because there was a lot of hope swirling around the nation." Although the country faced "growing pains and economic challenges," Devon eagerly anticipated starting school. There, he discovered his passion for soccer and began to develop a

"Improving your time management skills will allow you to prioritise your goals."

competitive nature. He explains, "The Jamaican education system is modelled after the British system, so there's a strong emphasis on competition, both in the classroom and on the soccer field. Competing in both arenas gave me a sense of validation."

Although his dream of becoming a soldier never wavered, he soon realised that as he got older, the competition in both the classroom and on the soccer field grew fiercer. He also became acutely aware of his family's poverty, especially when the lack of money for football boots meant he couldn't join the soccer games. Not wanting to be sidelined, he chose to take up running instead, stating, "Running didn't require shoes, so I started running track."

Inspired by Donald Quarrie's gold medal performance in the 200 metres at the 1976 Montreal Olympics, Devon began his training "in earnest." He remembers how a year before the 1979 Olympics, ABC Worldwide Sports aired a series called *Road to Moscow*, which featured athletes from around the globe sharing their "normal lives and the challenges they faced." Devon was struck by the athletes' "extraordinary dreams and their equally extraordinary drive to achieve them." This inspired him to train for the 1984 Olympics in Los Angeles. Recognising that sprinting was not his strength, he shifted his focus to middle-distance running, drawing motivation from his idols, Sebastian Coe, Steve Ovett, and Steve Cram.

Despite his growing passion for athletics, Devon always remembered his primary goal: enlisting in the army. So, after completing his A Levels, he applied to join the Jamaican Army as an Officer. The rigorous selection process involved a gruelling three-day series of eliminations among thirty-three candidates. Hailing from a part of Jamaica with limited opportunities for young men, Devon was determined to return home with success. The candidates were eventually narrowed down to nine, who were then taken to a training camp where they faced various challenges: a written test, an obstacle course, a mile run, a timed leadership exercise, and a speech. From this final group, only three were selected to become officers in training. Reflecting on the experience, Devon acknowledges, "It's the hardest thing I have ever had to do."

After enduring an intense training schedule, Devon boarded a plane for the first time in 1985, embarking on a long-haul flight to Sandhurst. He recalls, "It was a massive culture shock, going from Jamaica, where the population is 98% Black, to a place where almost everyone was white. I went from the heart of Jamaica to one of the most prestigious military training schools in the world." The cold weather, despite it being spring, was another jarring difference, but Devon was undeterred. He had a clear goal: to graduate and win the top overseas student award. "That was my sole purpose," he explains. Although he didn't secure the award, he did graduate and was commissioned just twelve days before his twenty-first birthday.

"Keep on pushing is about adapting."

Upon returning to Jamaica as a "young Black officer," Devon reflects on the challenges he faced, admitting he struggled with "organisational skills and time management." He also readily admits that as a young man, he could be quite stubborn. However, his biggest hurdle was that he found it difficult to shed the stigma associated with his origins. Despite his achievements, he felt that people treated him differently due to his background, sensing a pervasive lack of trust in his abilities. He explains, "They just wouldn't give me a chance."

For Devon, the army did not initially meet his childhood expectations. He recalls, "For the first eighteen months, I was miserable and frustrated. My confidence was at an all-time low; I couldn't seem to get anything right, and it felt like I was pushing a boulder uphill." Things began to improve only when a new company commander arrived who understood Devon's potential. But despite these challenges, Devon remained focused on his Olympic aspirations, continuing to train for the 1988 Korean Games.

Fortune seemed to smile on Devon during his unit's cross-country race when two Americans visited the Army seeking athletes to form a Jamaican bobsled team. Initially, around forty men expressed interest, but enthusiasm waned dramatically after they saw footage of "horrible crashes, blood everywhere, and people getting killed." By the next day, only about twenty men remained to try out for the team, and Devon emerged triumphant.

Devon finally reached the 1988 Winter Olympic Games held in Calgary, not as a driver but as a brakeman for the Jamaican bobsled team, which included Dudley Stokes, Michael White, Freddy Powell, and Chris Stokes. Interestingly, the team never owned their own bobsled; they rented it from the US and Canadian teams. Devon observes, "People will help you with almost anything during the Olympic Games, especially when you're seen as the underdogs from a tropical climate competing in winter sports." In their third run out of four, they lost control of the bobsled and crashed, failing to finish officially. Nevertheless, their remarkable story captured the world's imagination, and they returned to Jamaica as heroes.

Although they didn't win a medal, their story has become a beloved part of popular culture, inspiring songs, films, and video games. For Devon, however, the most enduring and poignant takeaway was the experience of participating in the Games itself. The journey and the opportunity to be there left a lasting impact beyond any medal.

Having mingled with people from all corners of the globe, Devon realised that "the only real differences between us are the ideologies we've been fed by others. We share similar dreams and aspirations and experience the same human fears. Fundamentally, we are much more alike than we are different." Devon views his

"Every goal you pursue will
have an obstacle in front of it."

Olympic experience as a pivotal "door opener." Now, at sixty, he is a sought-after motivational speaker with the mantra "Keep on Pushing." Drawing from his rich experiences, Devon sees life as a journey of "growth, transition, and adaptation."

A few years ago, Devon returned to his old neighbourhood and visited his primary school. Inspired by his experiences and discussions with the principal, he founded the Keep on Pushing Foundation. The foundation supports a breakfast club to ensure every child at the school receives a meal and a school bag filled with supplies. Additionally, it has established a wellness bay and set up a computer lab accessible to the students and the broader community. Having grown up in a deprived area of Jamaica, Devon viewed education as his "haven" and now strives to offer that same opportunity to others. His long-term vision is to extend the foundation's impact on a global scale.

From his beginnings in the "hood," Devon's life has been a testament to learning, perseverance, and overcoming challenges. Today, he finds fulfilment in his running, his role as a father, and his efforts to inspire others. Whether on the bobsled track or the speaking stage, he believes his true vocation has always been, and will remain, "challenging and inspiring people to reach their fullest potential and to make a tangible impact."

"Treat others as you allow them to treat you. Be humble. Be kind. Be ambitious."

HOW TO SURVIVE AND THRIVE

VOLUME II

VOLKER JAECKEL

Founder and President of Coaching Formula LLC d/b/a FocalPoint Business Coaching and Training, Temecula Valley, California

Volker Jaeckel

As a schoolboy high jumper and footballer, Volker's passion for sports has never wavered. When he opened his own sportswear shop in 1995, despite facing resistance, it was no surprise that he chose to stock his favourite brand, Reebok. It's also interesting to note that during his visits to the Reebok showroom to order new collections, he often saw the iconic Shaquille O'Neal's Reebok shoes, size 22, a testament to the largest feet ever seen on a pro basketball court. Reebok is not the only passion we have shared, as speaking with Volker revealed that we have much in common; we both support Liverpool FC, admire Winston Churchill, and shared a relentless determination in our business endeavours.

Volker grew up in Düsseldorf, Germany, raised by modest parents who had first-hand experience of the horrors of World War II. His father, once a promising footballer, was conscripted into the military at the age of seventeen and tragically lost his leg in battle. Volker's father's future changed direction. His football days were unfortunately over, so he decided to train as a carpenter. Volker's mother supplemented the family income by cleaning offices, and as a child, Volker learned early on that he needed to help the family, and so during school holidays, he would often go with his mother to clean offices.

"When you think you can do it. Do it. Don't let yourself get diminished by naysayers."

Instead of pursuing a university education, Volker chose to complete an apprenticeship in sales before joining the army in 1986. As a Staff Sergeant in the German Armed Forces Military Police, he was responsible for leading a team of eight soldiers, a role that instilled in him valuable leadership skills. By 1990, around the time of German reunification, Volker decided to transition into a career in pharmaceutical sales. He explains his decision to diversify, "I always looked around the fence, over the fence, or around the corner to see what else is there."

Ten years later, at the age of thirty-six, Volker's life changed direction again. He got divorced, sold all his belongings, and left Germany. He headed for America with $1000, a suitcase, and one box of sales books in German from business guru and self-development expert Brian Tracy, "who was, and still is, a dear friend."

With limited English, Volker secured a job selling steel, a position that required him to make a 180-mile round trip to work each day. Despite his dedication, he faced suspicion and hesitation from others in the aftermath of the 9/11 attacks, as Volker recalls, "People were still hesitant to hire foreigners." His persistence eventually paid off when he approached an important dealership selling German cars with the pitch, "Mr Williams, I think it makes sense to have a German guy, with a German accent, selling your German cars." The owner took a chance on him, and Volker went on to become one of the top 20 performers in customer satisfaction from New York to Wisconsin in less than eight months.

"You can always do more than you think you can."

However, while working in the car showroom in 2002, Volker's life changed forever when he received the devastating news that his four-month-old son, Nicholas, had passed away from sudden infant death syndrome. Volker believes that his ability to carry on is rooted in the conviction that his son has been guiding him ever since. He also credits his success to his resilience, stating that "nothing can rattle me any longer." This profound loss has given him an unshakable strength that has carried him through the challenges of life and business.

A year later, Volker found himself in the right place at the right time and seized the opportunity presented by the growing trend of online shopping. In 2003, when online car sales were still relatively new, Volker recognised its potential as the future of e-commerce. He developed innovative marketing initiatives and processes to boost sales, such as sending out videos to prospective clients, a novelty at this time. His forward-thinking approach paid off, earning him a spot on the front cover of *Digital Dealer Magazine* as one of the top 10 e-commerce directors in the United States by 2009.

In 2014, Volker published his book, *The Digital Dealership: A Battle-Worn Roadmap to Online Success*, sharing his insights and experiences in the evolving world of online sales. Following this achievement, he was hired by software service company Cobalt as a digital marketing ambassador. In this role, he travelled across the United States, speaking at conferences to dealership groups and OEMs, spreading what he called the "gospel of digital marketing," and helping businesses adapt to the digital age.

In 2018, Volker was invited to speak before a thousand executives in Milan, Italy, on the topic of 'What will the future of automotive retail look like?' His presentation included the rise of a new medium, artificial intelligence, and how it would become an essential element of business marketing in the future. Volker emphasises that AI shouldn't be used "on autopilot, you still have to prompt engineer and steer it, but it's a blessing in disguise for many marketers." His key advice is to "make AI your friend, assistant, and colleague," recognising its potential to transform marketing strategies when used effectively.

In 2020, Volker started as the Chief Marketing Officer for Unstoppable Automotive Group. It was during COVID, and although nobody was buying cars, Volker explains, "I just turned the marketing around and based on the procedures I created, in just three to five months, we were one of the few selling and servicing cars, despite the government implementing restraints on how car shoppers could obtain vehicles. We were the only Mercedes-Benz franchise in the world that grew traffic and sales by +30% during this time." While every other franchise was stagnating, his growth caught the attention of the CEO of Mercedes-Benz, who visited Volker in California to figure out what he was doing differently.

"Everything is a process."

During his time in pharmaceutical sales, Volker observed that pharmacists in Germany held a status similar to that of doctors. He notes, "They were very smart, very precise, and sometimes arrogant." Each time he walked into a pharmacy, he was often met with the same dismissive response, "We don't need anything." However, as a trained salesperson, Volker knew not to take no for an answer. He relied on his emotional intelligence to read their behavioural responses and adjusted his pitches accordingly, often turning initial resistance into a successful sale.

Having been in business for forty years, Volker has "learned about empathy, how to speak to people and how to lead by implementing the Platinum Rule," which he operates in his business coaching firm. The Platinum Rule states, "Don't speak to people how you would like to be spoken to, but instead speak to them how they would like to be spoken to." He has also learned a lot about the mechanics of business, and as a certified business coach, he emphasises the importance of emotional intelligence. He defines it as "the ability to recognise, understand, influence, guide, and manage both your own emotions and those of others." This unique skill continues to be invaluable, allowing him to "read the room and sense the emotions in it."

As a business executive coach, Volker uses the DISC model (Dominance, Influence, Steadiness, and Conscientiousness) to conduct in-depth behavioural assessments. This method allows him to analyse people by observing their behaviour, mannerisms, and even the way their workspaces are organised. Through these observations, he gains valuable insights into their personalities, communication styles, and how they interact with others, enabling him to tailor his coaching to meet their individual needs.

The DISC model is represented as a circular chart, with each quadrant leaning toward a specific colour—red, yellow, green, or blue—based on the findings. These colours correspond to different personality traits: red signifies competitiveness, yellow reflects enthusiasm and sociability, green emphasises building relationships and harmony, and blue indicates a focus on accuracy and precision. Analysing his own personality traits, Volker acknowledges that he identifies as predominantly "red." However, over time, he has been able to master the art of DISC to become adaptable and now sees himself as a "learning chameleon."

Volker also developed a Communication Breakthrough Program, which is now implemented at California State University and the School of Entrepreneurship.

"When you think you can't—you can. You just have to shift approach."

This program is used to teach classes on behavioural assessment, helping students understand and apply the DISC framework in real-world scenarios.

It's easy to see why his mentor and longstanding friend Brian Tracy has been such an influence in Volker's life. He values integrity, and and says that Brian Tracy, the self-development guru, who has written over seventy books, has "always been true to himself." That is what Volker admires in others. He also suggests that if everyone could cultivate a bit more compassion and understanding for others' perspectives, we would all be better off.

In 2022, he faced a life-threatening battle with sepsis, coming within "two hours of death." To celebrate his recovery and finally start ticking off his 'bucket list,' he flew to England to watch his beloved Liverpool play West Ham in London. The icing on the cake? Liverpool won 2-1. At sixty, Volker shows no signs of slowing down. After spending the past twenty-three years in America, he's eager to expand his coaching and speaking business into Europe, Australia, and "worldwide."

As a business coach, Volker emphasises the importance of attentive listening, always arriving on time, under-promising and over-delivering, observing carefully, and consistently following up. His core message boils down to one word, "respect." He also highlights the value of tenacity, which he feels has become a "lost art" for many, particularly among today's youth, whom he refers to as the "entitlement generation" because of their expectation of instant results. While he acknowledges that young people still have dreams and ambitions, he notes, "They want it now."

Volker is a passionate amateur photographer, an avid reader, and a self-described "complex thinker." He dreams in vivid images and visualises what he wants to see unfold in the future. He believes this imaginative process, which is also known as "The Law of Attraction," is a key factor in maintaining his good mental health. Although he feels ready to pursue global expansion, Volker is grateful for the many opportunities America has provided him. Now, with seven children and his life partner, Snowwhite, of thirteen years, he reflects on his journey so far. From being the shortest boy in school who went on to win the high jump competition to making it on the front cover of a business magazine, writing a book, speaking in front of thousands of business professionals, becoming a sought-after business coach, and most recently being nominated for The Spirit of the Entrepreneur Award in Riverside County, California. At this stage in his life, Volker takes pride in his accomplishments while eagerly anticipating the exciting possibilities that lie ahead.

> "Make your disadvantages
> play to your advantage."

"Listening is everything."

HOW TO
SURVIVE
AND
THRIVE
VOLUME II

ABRAHAM CHARLES

Founder and CEO of each&everyone, Social Influencer Agency, International Speaker, Investor

Abraham Charles

Abraham Charles and I both come from sport-loving households. In my family, we didn't just make running shoes; we also participated in the sport. I remember, when I was younger, winning a dictionary in a running competition. At the time, I was massively disappointed, as I really wanted a football, but decades later, it was that very same dictionary that I referred to when searching for the Reebok name. It seemed like this was my destiny, similar to Abraham, who eventually became the founder and CEO of his own social influencer agency after years of trial and error.

Abraham had an unconventional childhood growing up in an inner-city suburb in Leeds; he describes a life of contradiction and opportunity. Although based in Little London, Leeds, with its poverty and gang activity, Abraham had a far from deprived upbringing. Being part of a "close-knit" family of more than forty cousins, he had the immeasurable benefit of positive role models, many of whom shared his passion and talent for playing football.

As the only Black student in a private school, Abraham struggled to be accepted by his peers, and as the only boy going to school wearing a bright blue, red, and white pinstripe blazer with grey shorts and socks, he also struggled to be accepted within his wider community.

255

His passion for football helped keep him off the streets, away from the gangs and on a more productive path. He dreamed of following in some of his relatives' footsteps and playing football professionally. However, several injuries, along with his parents' determination for him to settle into a secure job, prevented Abraham from pursuing the sport to a higher level. It was a practical decision that changed his life trajectory, and one that, despite all of his success, is still something that he slightly regrets to this day.

Being practical was at the very heart of his upbringing. While running his upholstery business, Abraham's father insisted that his son go to work on Saturday and Sunday mornings, sweeping the workshop floor, salvaging any surplus material, then sorting out the cloth by colour to make buttons. After a hard week at school, while most teenagers were spending their weekends playing video games, watching TV, or being with friends, Abraham was learning about hard work and self-discipline.

His private education afforded him a range of opportunities that widened his worldview; he played golf, went skiing, and travelled internationally on school trips. It also gave him the impression that his father, who came to the UK as a five-year-old from the West Indies, was a rich man.

"Build a connection, and build trust."

As he grew up, his father diversified into owning restaurants and nightclubs and exposed Abraham to a new type of business. On the opening night of their first club, NATO, Abraham recalls there was a queue of tens of thousands of people for a club with a capacity of 2000. Working in one of the most popular club destinations in the mid-nineties, Abraham was meeting a stream of celebrities and developing a talent for planning music events. However, the glitz and glamour had a darker side, and when Abraham's father came up against racketeering, things became violent and threatening, and so he returned to working in the upholstery business.

Afterwards, Abraham went to university to study business and accounting. However, his passion for music and events resurfaced a few years later when he created a nightclub called Fibre with his father. After five years of success, Abraham went on to explore other avenues. He first created an app that allowed clients to book tables in bars, get VIP access, and order food and drinks using the POS systems. He then later sold this technology to be used in amusement parks as a way to fast-track rides.

After gaining directorship experience in several areas relating to digital consultancy, PR, and marketing, Abraham developed a formula that allowed him "to analyse social accounts and the influence it had on the followers of those social accounts." This led him to found his own company, each&everyone, an influencer marketing agency that aims to connect brands with influencers as a marketing strategy. Abraham found that, with their permission, he could analyse data, as well as look at the e-commerce systems His "bespoke analysis tool that crunched campaign data, allowed me to connect to the influencers' social handles across Facebook, Instagram, TikTok, and YouTube." He explains how "all of that alignment allowed [them] to look at historical trends, then predict a forecast of what the campaign output should be. And ultimately, my goal is to drive an ROI, which turns into monetary value."

The tough lessons Abraham learned starting each&everyone really shaped him into the successful entrepreneur he is today. He recalls a moment he came close to bankruptcy due to incompetence in lead generation and finances. He discovered he had far less money than he was led to believe, and the three-month leads were, in fact, two years down the pipeline—too long to stay afloat. With a young family, he was "48 hours to the breadline with a business that was going under." He sold his car and took out a personal loan just to pay the wages. After days calling everyone and anyone, he was given a lifeline, "a two-week deal just to get £3000 in the bank account." The two-week deal turned into a month, then three months, and now twelve. Abraham learned an invaluable lesson about cash flow, as he now knows "when to make payments, when to hold payments back, when to ask for money from clients, and how to structure contracts in terms of how much they should be paying up front." However, above all, he explains, "The biggest lesson I've learned so far is that I ask for full payment upfront, and get the revenue in as quickly as possible."

For Abraham, what sets each&everyone apart from their competitors is being "agnostic to utilising any influencer." He suggests that other companies have a roster of influencers on their books, whereas Abraham "reverse engineers the process." He initially gets to understand the brand and the business KPIs. Abraham's company will look at details like price points and distribution and identify competitors and their price points. They also perform a detailed analysis of vanity metrics such as follow ratios, engagement rates, content formats, narrative and tone of voice and much more to carefully select influencers for specific brand campaigns.

The information is interpreted into a score rating system, and the highest achieving influencers would be put forward for a campaign, doing five posts, which could be a brand uplift, traffic to a landing page, or just contributing to a general sentiment. He's so confident about his analysis tool that he is able to guarantee the predicted ROI with a money-back guarantee.

Abraham's work focuses on influencers, and he sees his company at some stage moving more towards AI influencers who can "multitask 24/7." He "[sees] it as being the future; everything is turning into the digital world, the Metaverse. For example, digital AI influencers can be a part of that world and be able to sell and advise people on which worlds to buy into and who best to interact with."

It's another topic that Abraham appears passionate about, to the extent that he is currently in conversation with some developers about turning himself into an avatar and an AI proposition. Abraham explains, "I could be my own AI brand out in the ecosystem and turn myself into a digital influencer." To achieve this, Abraham is currently cloning his own voice and facial recognition so that he can reach a larger, more diverse audience quicker. As an avatar, he would be able to speak in different languages, as well as have the ability to scan and "repurpose" other influencers for various regions and multipurpose campaigns. He "[believes] it's the future. AI, itself, is making the creative world speed up a hell of a lot quicker than what it used to be." Despite that observation, Abraham insists that "it's a tool to enhance creativity, but it's not the be-all-and-end-all because you need the physical mind and the back and forth of collaboration to come up with different ideas."

Building on his passion for AI, his new venture, AIRO Technology, is transforming the business of indoor air quality management. The company employs cutting-edge, patented solutions to enhance both health and efficiency in commercial and residential spaces.

AIRO's flagship innovation, the "world's first ductwork deposit monitoring sensor," offers unparalleled precision in measuring dust and grease deposits in HVAC systems at the micron level. This technology not only optimises system performance but also ensures cleaning only occurs when necessary, thereby reducing energy consumption.

"As long as the staff are happy,
the company will grow."

The AI-powered AirVision technology detects a wide range of airborne pollutants, including gases, dust, pollen, and other contaminants. This advanced monitoring system is ideal for diverse environments, from public spaces and office buildings to commercial outlets and healthcare facilities. By improving air quality, it can boost employee productivity and mitigate health risks associated with poor indoor air conditions.

For home use, the AirVision Home provides a sleek, portable solution for monitoring personal air quality. Equipped with a user-friendly mobile app, it tracks temperature, humidity, and pollutants, making it an essential tool for the health-conscious homeowner.

Like many, Abraham is eager to embrace AI technology, but he is also wary of the possible ramifications, suggesting the need for an "intermediary protocol." As a contented forty-three-year-old father of two, Abraham feels he is still striving for happiness and would like to have more of a work-life balance. He also meditates "just to bring [his] own internal system to a stable level."

His advice to "never give up" is popular amongst successful entrepreneurs, but he's also a great believer in face-to-face communication, suggesting that there's only so far you can go with emails and phone calls. Abraham has come a long way from the quiet schoolboy who never quite felt like he fit in. One minute he was rubbing shoulders with boys who were being picked up at school in their parents' Lamborghinis, Rolls-Royces, and even helicopters, and the next minute, he'd be dodging local gangs hanging around the street corners of Leeds.

Perhaps it's this mix of privilege and difficulty, success and failure, expectations and disappointments that has formed Abraham's perspective on life and business. A natural connector, he is a strong networker and tech-savvy entrepreneur. With a wide range of passions and talents, he could easily have had a number of successful careers, yet his strong work ethic allowed him to ride the waves of adversity and succeed no matter what.

"Always be on time. If you can't be on time, be early, and if you're on time, you're late."

HOW TO
SURVIVE
AND
THRIVE

VOLUME II

Let's share wisdom!

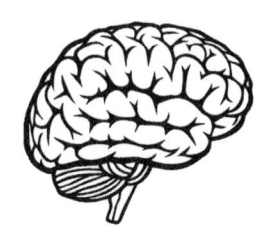

"It's easy to think about what sector you should be in and what function or what role. But also think about what stage of the organisation you want to be in. Try each stage to see where you're the happiest."

Matt Van Itallie
Founder and CEO of Sema

"If you want to dream impossibly big goals, be bold."

Michael B. Clegg
Leadership Coach and Keynote Speaker

"Cravings are not a negative nuisance. Tune into them to gain insight into yourself and your desires. This will help you to live authentically."

Meribel Goldwin
Founder of Blossomed Life LLC

"Be thankful for moments where you get to pause. Whether it's family commitments, traffic, or having no Wi-Fi on a plane, use these opportunities to re-energise yourself."

Max Rivera
Global Partnerships at Snap Inc.

"100% of successful people just do stuff. They don't talk about it. Just get out there and do it."

Michael Dargie
Founder of Make More Creative

"Let go of the need for toxic perfectionism and learn to embrace your imperfections as you strive for excellence with greater kindness and compassion for yourself and others."

Michele Molitor
Confidence Coach and Hypnotherapist for Nectar Consulting Inc.

"Self-care is important. It's difficult to help others if you're not taking care of yourself."

Nafisa Shehu
Speech and Language Therapist

"Listen more than you talk. Listen to the feedback of your team members, listen to the feedback of your employees, and use that feedback to continuously improve your services and product."

Natalia Grozina
Founder of Grozina

"Achieving success in a company is about alignment. Get everyone on board with the idea and be really clear about each person's role so that everyone is rowing in the same direction towards success."

Nikhil Vaish
CEO and Founder of BoostSolo

"Continue learning, improving, and being alert to what's happening around you."

Nathan Clements
Partner of The Alexander Partnership

"Dream big, and when you dream big, believe in that dream. Then, be sure to prepare for it because it will, in fact, happen."

Netta Jenkins
CEO of Aerodei

"People who share love, care, and support will help you feel safe enough to take the risks that your success will require. As you pursue your dreams, be that positive person for others."

Nola Saint James
Author

"Never confuse your perspective
with other people's perception."

Nicci Take
Global Deal Coach at Mercer

"Saying thank you is transformative.
Let it resonate within your body and
let it radiate out."

Patricia Perez
Coach at Talaya Guides

"Embrace failure. We learn from it, we
understand more because of it, and we
appreciate our success because of it."

Patrick Riccards
CEO of the Driving Force Institute for Public Engagement

"Don't think of how to do it alone. Think of who to do it with."

Odera Nonyelu Ume-Ezeoke
Founder of Limbic Capital

"We can't go it alone. Surround yourself with others who are on a good path and who can lift you up. Life will be so much richer."

Paul Kirch
Founder of BOSS Academy Community

"People believe 20% of what you tell them and 80% of what you show them. So the more visual you can be, the better."

Paul Meek
Financial Planner

"If you don't like where you are, move.
You're not a tree."

Peter Shankman
Author and Keynote Speaker

"The more you help others, the
happier you are. Just think with
your heart and open your arms."

Peter Jumrukovski
Real Estate Agent

"Who dares, wins, and the only way to achieve
the impossible is to believe it is possible."

Ofir Dagan
Co-Founder and CEO of Movmenta

"Fail fast. Fail cheap.
Keep trying."

Peter Moore
Former CEO of Liverpool Football Club

"Block out the noise and stay faithful to your true self. Go for it with everything you've got."

Paul Williams
Brand strategist and CEO of Spearhead Creativity

"Sit down with yourself and listen to the quiet voices inside that tell you what you want and need."

Rikard Karlsson
Author, Speaker and Vascular Surgeon

"Call a spade a spade and
live your truth."

Ray Doustdar
Host of Deep Shallow Dive Podcast

"Competition is irrelevant. If you want to make something extraordinary that nobody has ever done before, you cannot look to other people, other companies, or other leaders as examples."

Robert Lennox
Business Consultant and Coach

"Get yourself some quick
wins and build from there."

Robert Smith
Founder of Smith Prophets

"The human brain wants to feel challenged, respected, and valued. If you make your team feel these three things, you're not managing; you're leading."

Rob Gaedtke
President and CEO of KPS3

"Always bet on yourself. Trust your abilities, your instincts, and your decision-making, even when things seem stacked against you."

Taylor Green
Founder and CEO of TAG Media Agency

"If you want to rise, talk about your work at a higher altitude."

Tom Henschel
Executive Coach

INDIRA NICOLE PERSAD, PhD

CEO of ActionEDGE TT

Indira Nicole Persad, PhD

In March 2020, just as the world began to confront lockdown restrictions, Indira launched a webinar, coincidentally titled *Survive and Thrive*. It was an initiative remarkably attuned to the times, resonating with those striving to navigate the complex challenges of the pandemic. Our discussion revealed not only the resilience essential for weathering such unprecedented events but also the innovative strategies she employed to not merely survive but even thrive beyond those dark days.

Indira Nicole Persad's name is a vibrant tapestry of her Indo-Caribbean heritage. It carries the powerful legacy of Indira Gandhi, India's first and only female prime minister, and the lively spirit of Nicole, a Trinidad and Tobago carnival queen. This unique blend of political strength and Caribbean vibrancy perfectly captures the richness and complexity of her identity. Indira explains that this dual heritage has profoundly shaped her perspective, allowing her to draw from two distinct traditions to cultivate a deep sense of belonging and purpose.

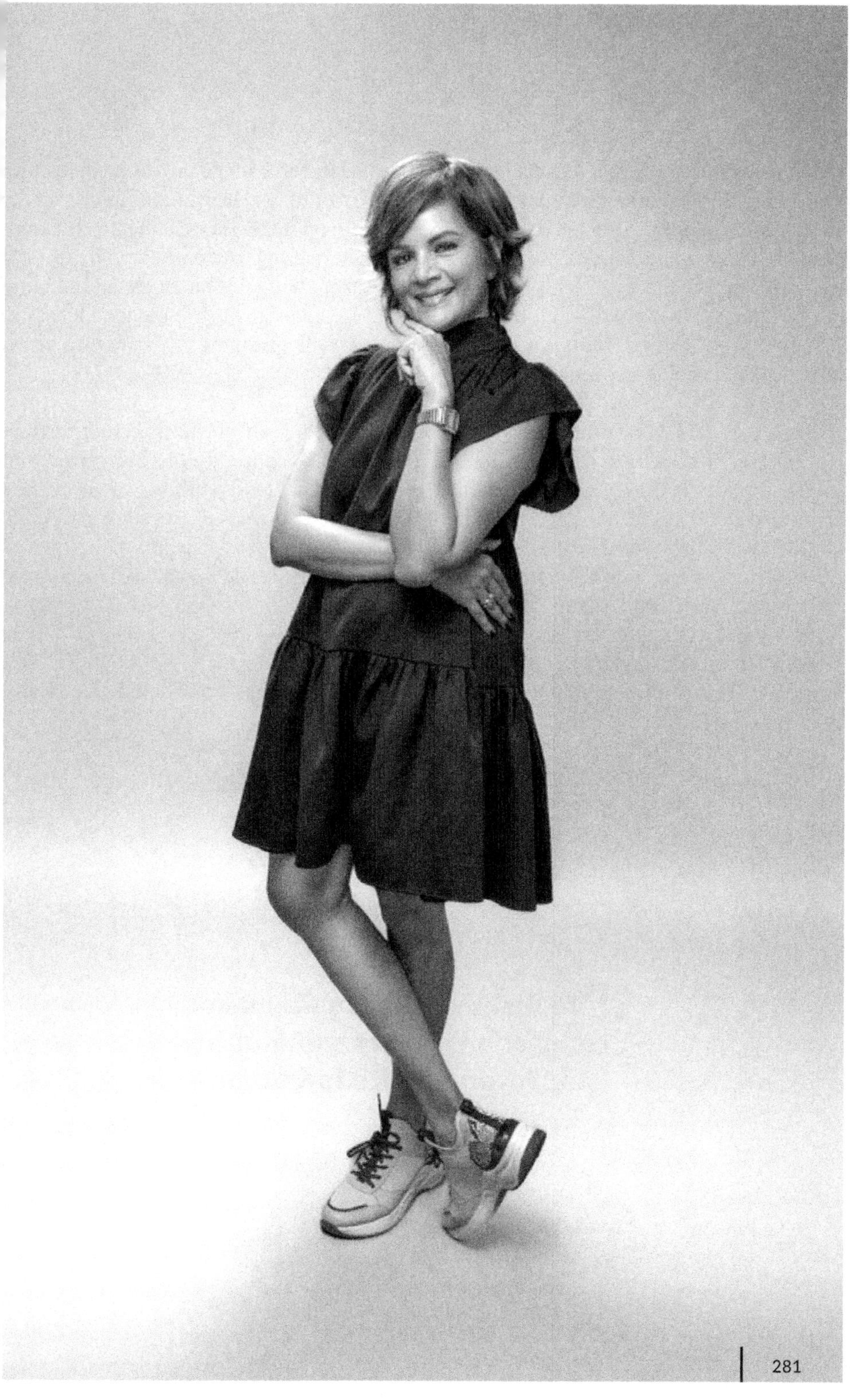

Indira reflects that her resilience and strength can be traced back to her deep connection with her entrepreneurial grandmother, Joan (Chanarjotie), and her mother, Joyce. In the 1940s, when society expected women to focus solely on motherhood and homemaking, Joan defied conventions. She wore her Hindu head covering, or "ohrni," while driving a car, raising her family, working alongside her husband in their business, and sending her five daughters abroad—to India, the UK, and Ireland—to pursue higher education. Joyce, in turn, instilled in Indira a spirit of courage and adventure, encouraging her to embrace new challenges and explore without fear.

Indira's parents—her Hindu father and Christian mother—were unwavering in their commitment to ensuring their children received the best education possible. However, Indira found the local educational system uninspiring and stifling, often feeling scrutinised and restricted. It wasn't until she moved to the UK to study at Royal Holloway College that her true academic journey began. This was an era before the ease of modern communication, and for the first time, she found herself distanced from her family. During this period, she had one of her first 'survive and thrive' moments. Rather than dwelling on the separation, she focused on the vibrant, diverse environment around her, which sparked her curiosity. Immersed in new perspectives, she developed a passion for learning and began exploring social issues that would ultimately shape her future career.

> **"To thrive, build bonds, make connections, foster community, and leverage with intention."**

Indira's time in the UK was deeply transformative. The anonymity of her new environment provided her with the freedom to explore her identity and connect with truly inspiring, kind individuals who accepted her for who she was. Unlike her peers, many of whom followed traditional paths such as marriage or pursued professions like law, medicine, engineering, or teaching, Indira began to envisage a clear direction for herself, one that aligned with her deeper purpose: to inspire others to be more, do more, and have more.

With a strong social conscience and a passion for empowering others, she sought roles that allowed her to write about, support, and advocate for social change and conflict resolution. She also embraced her desire to celebrate women, writing articles on women in the workforce and forging connections with other women who were championing equality.

As her visa expiration drew near, she enrolled in a PhD programme, where she explored "the role that NGOs play in improving living conditions for people in Jamaica." As part of her research, she traded Britain's grey skies for the sunny shores of Jamaica. Jamaica had a reputation for being challenging and occasionally dangerous, a notion that sent her parents into a frenzy when they learned she was moving there. But for Indira, it was exactly what she needed—a chance to recharge and reconnect with her "passion for life."

Indira vividly remembers her arrival in Kingston in the mid-1990s, a time when she had to "find her way," build resilience, and strengthen her mental fortitude. Jamaica, in stark contrast to the overwhelming abundance of the UK, offered a refreshing simplicity. Shopping for essentials meant choosing from just one type of bread or a single brand of laundry detergent. This simplicity, however, proved to be liberating and became a defining aspect of her journey. Free from the burden of endless choices and "decision fatigue," life in Jamaica brought her a sense of clarity and focus, allowing her to fully immerse herself in her work and environment.

She fondly recalls the moment she decided to move to Jamaica: sitting on a street, enjoying a delicious "steamed fish" and a cold beer, with the sun warming her back. At that moment, she realised she had rediscovered her appreciation for the simple pleasures in life.

"Change your view, and a new world will open to you."

In Jamaica, Indira witnessed the impact of socio-economic challenges up close. The clear contrast between the resources available in the UK and Jamaica highlighted the incredible resilience of communities that thrived through unity and ingenuity despite having limited options. This experience was a profound lesson for her, teaching her the immense value of community-driven solutions. Along her journey, she encountered strong female mentors who took her under their wing, including the late Jacqueline da Costa, who at the time was Senior Advisor to the Prime Minister on Land Policy.

Indira's path took an exciting turn when she secured a role with the Inter-American Development Bank. Here, she experienced a moment that would shape her future. Tasked with assessing the feasibility of a new community centre in a rural area, she quickly realised that what the locals truly needed wasn't a new facility but rather essential skills like parenting. This disconnect between what was planned and what was actually needed left her disillusioned and frustrated by the lack of tangible impact she could make within the system. Reflecting on that period, she fondly recalls, "I created a wonderful network of friends. It was a fantastic experience, learning and understanding the world beyond the textbook, but I realised it was too political, so I had to find another way to make a difference."

Driven by a passion for creating real change, Indira boldly decided to leave the bank and launch her own venture. With her husband, David Couch, she co-founded Produce to Products Ltd, a company dedicated to transforming Jamaican produce into value-added goods. Inspired by her mother-in-law's delicious chutneys made from local fruits and spices, Indira sought to turn raw resources into marketable products. This venture not only provided employment for local communities but also promoted financial independence for its staff and fostered sustainable growth for the business.

Sometimes, life takes you on unexpected journeys, as Indira discovered when her dear friend Erin Chang handed her a copy of *The Secrets of a Millionaire Mindset*. The back cover invited readers to a workshop in the US, which Indira attended with Erin.

"The more we collaborate, the more we can ideate."

She describes the workshop as a "boot camp" that posed a thought-provoking question: "If you had all the money in the world, what would you do?" Her answer, though simple, was profound: to travel more and fix the road in her neighbourhood. This "lightbulb" moment revealed to Indira her self-limiting beliefs around money, opening her eyes to new possibilities.

After that realisation, Indira returned to Jamaica with a renewed sense of purpose, determined to "take this business and do things differently." She made the decision to "get out of her own way," focus on building stronger relationships, and join various associations to connect with like-minded business owners. Despite operating in a "male-dominated environment," she eventually rose to the position of Director at the Jamaica Manufacturers and Exporters Association with the support of the late Sameer Younis. During this time, she also gained invaluable guidance from powerful female mentors like Doreen Frankson. Indira looks back on this period as one of significant personal growth, as she learned to navigate business challenges in ways that brought her closer to her vision and goals.

Indira's journey was never without its hurdles. The devaluation of the dollar made borrowing expensive, but her ability to connect with people and leverage relationships proved to be her greatest asset. Through strategic networking and outreach, she secured loans and grants that gradually helped her business gain momentum. Understanding the importance of finance, accounting, and marketing, she threw herself into learning how to make informed business decisions. All the while, she skillfully navigated the complexities of running a business, steadily building a foundation for long-term success.

Indira Nicole Persad, PhD

Indira's multifaceted approach has been the key to her growth, enabling her to build a solid foundation for her business. She takes great pride in treating her employees fairly and respectfully, empowering them to develop their skills and improve their lives. For Indira, her business is far more than just a venture; it is a meaningful way to contribute to society positively. While she recognises that she cannot change the world on her own, she finds deep fulfillment in knowing she can have a significant impact on people's lives through the employment opportunities she provides.

In 2007, Produce to Products ceased manufacturing after concluding a royalty deal. Inspired by T. Harv Eker's focus on "passive income streams," Indira sold her recipe to a well-known local Jamaican company, Pickapeppa. Reflecting on this transition, she emphasises the importance of financial independence, seeing it as a platform that enables her to focus on more community-driven initiatives and projects.

Indira has returned to Trinidad and Tobago, where she now serves as the CEO of *Action Edge TT*, a company that offers business coaching and consulting services to help individuals and organisations achieve peak performance. As a serial entrepreneur with a talent for problem-solving, she has also expanded into a partnership in a salon and spa business in Guyana.

Indira's personal philosophy as an entrepreneur is centred around identifying and solving problems, with profits being a natural outcome of creating meaningful solutions. Her approach goes beyond financial success; it involves generating employment, ensuring fair wages, promoting employee welfare, and fostering financial independence. She is particularly passionate about upskilling, especially for women, and believes in equipping individuals with the tools they need to thrive both professionally and personally.

In her business ventures, Indira sees herself as a "transformational leader." She focuses on hiring individuals based on their alignment with core values—such as abundance, innovation, resilience, commitment, agility, and fun—rather than on their personality alone. Indira believes that if candidates embody these values, they can be trained in the technical skills required for the job. To assess this alignment, she presents candidates with real-world scenarios that reflect the company's values, helping her evaluate their fit with the organisation. This values-driven leadership has been key to creating a supportive and dynamic workplace culture.

Her progressive approach to leadership and management has enabled her team to adapt to the evolving work environment, demonstrating that productivity flourishes when employees are empowered.

A strong advocate for remote work, Indira recognises the growing frustration employees feel with long commutes. She stresses the importance for leaders to "adjust their gaze" and rethink their approach to remote and hybrid work models. Indira believes in fostering a culture of flexibility and trust, which she sees as essential for boosting both morale and productivity. Confident in the success of remote work when done strategically, she emphasises the need for cohesive communication and team engagement as the foundation for success in a remote or hybrid setting.

With a young adult son and daughter, Indira looks forward to mentoring young women, helping them "understand the importance of financial independence and making sound, thoughtful decisions." Drawing inspiration from her own journey, she hopes to empower the next generation to embrace their potential and create fulfilling futures for themselves.

Indira sees herself as a dynamic serial entrepreneur and encourages others to adopt a growth mindset, always seeking opportunities, even in the face of adversity. She believes that challenging societal norms, building a strong network of like-minded individuals, and continuously investing in personal development have been key to her success. With a wealth of ideas, she is eager to explore business opportunities that highlight the unique culture and traditions of the Caribbean.

Indira also believes that happiness is a choice, and she takes mindful steps each day to make that choice. To maintain her energy, she is selective about the information she consumes, avoiding "energy vampires" and surrounding herself with supportive, inspiring individuals who bring out the best in her. She remains mindful of her emotional triggers, and her daily routine prioritises quality sleep, exercise, meditation, and a balanced diet. Indira's approach to self-care is rooted in the belief that inner peace and resilience are crucial to living a fulfilling, purposeful life.

"Be mindful of where your
time and energy flow. What
you put in is what will grow."

HOW TO SURVIVE AND THRIVE

VOLUME II

MIKE RADOOR
Co-founder of miinto.com

Mike Radoor

A t the end of my interview with Mike, he posed a thought-provoking question: "As a leader of a global brand, what do you consider your most valuable trait?" Without thinking, I immediately replied, "You have to listen." During my years at Reebok, with all its highs and lows, I always prioritised listening. I firmly believe that if you're the one doing all the talking, you're not learning. Even now, after listening to Mike's fantastic insights, I can confidently say I've learned something new. It's a reminder that no matter how much experience you have, there's always more to learn—especially from the next generation of innovators.

Mike was born and raised in Odense, Denmark, in a working-class neighborhood he calls a "mini ghetto." Despite the rough environment, or perhaps because of it, Mike was always outspoken and willing to stand up for what he believed in. This trait often got him into trouble, but it also set the stage for the person he would become—a fighter who was never willing to back down.

At the time, Mike's father had undiagnosed bipolar disorder, which frequently disrupted the family's stability with his unpredictable manic episodes. Mike vividly remembers one particular incident when he came home crying after a fight with a boy who had wrecked his bike. His nose was bloodied, so his father took him to the neighbour's house. When the boy's father answered the door, Mike's dad simply stated that while it was acceptable for his son to beat Mike, destroying his bike was crossing a line—because it cost money.

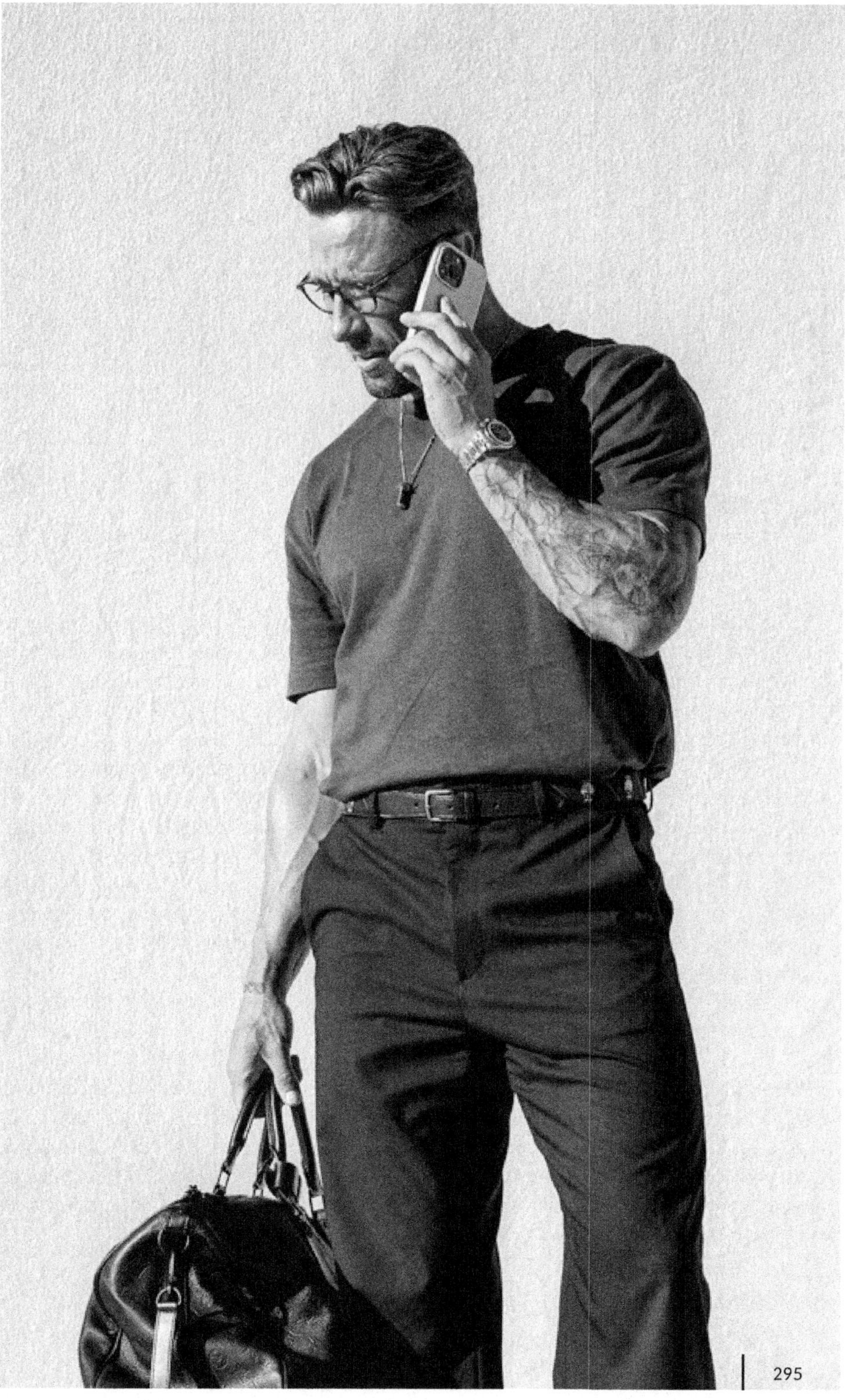

When Mike was about eight, they moved from the estate to a nearby villa, ushering in a short period of stability for the family. However, one pivotal moment from this time remains vivid in Mike's memory. He had returned to the estate to visit a friend for a chess game, playing for pennies. After losing all his money, Mike refused to hand it over and quickly escaped on rollerblades. In his haste, he crossed a busy road and was struck by a car travelling at around 50 mph. The impact was catastrophic—Mike suffered a badly broken leg, severe facial injuries, and fell into a coma for two weeks. Due to the severity of his injuries, doctors warned Mike's parents that he might never play football again, and they also cautioned that his cognitive abilities could be affected. The news was devastating for Mike. However, when he returned to school, football in hand, he was determined to prove them wrong. Refusing to accept their prognosis, he continued kicking the ball around, pushing his limits. For the first time, he also began diligently doing his homework, determined not to fall behind. At just ten years old, Mike experienced a significant turning point, discovering the true power of determination and resilience.

However, while Mike was finding success at school, his home life was unravelling. His parents eventually separated, and his mother, then thirty-seven, moved her twenty-two-year-old boyfriend into their family home. Financial pressures quickly mounted, and they could no longer afford to stay. So, faced with limited options, Mike's mother moved into a small flat with her boyfriend, leaving Mike to live with his grandparents while his sister moved in with friends.

"It was a really tough period," Mike recalls. "I moved away from my school, my environment, and found myself alone with no friends." The sudden upheaval from everything familiar at such a crucial time in his life was profoundly challenging, isolating him from the social and emotional support he could once rely on.

As the new boy at school, Mike quickly became a target for bullies. He vividly remembers one winter day when the snow had piled high, and he knew the older boys would try to drag him off to rub his face in the freezing ice. Determined not to let it happen, Mike came to school prepared, packing his bag with "ice-hard snowballs." When the moment came, instead of surrendering, he fought back. His defiance caught them off guard, and from that day forward, Mike vowed never to be a victim again.

Mike's passion for football continued at this new school, and his hard work paid off when he was scouted by clubs just beneath the top divisions. But even as he achieved success on the field, emotional struggles continued. During one match, he overheard parents gossiping about his father's mental health. The unfairness of their comments enraged Mike, but rather than react outwardly, he used his anger to fuel his performance. He scored five goals and, with twenty minutes still left on the clock, walked off the pitch to be with his father, a silent protest against the injustice he couldn't accept.

At twenty-one, Mike decided not to pursue a football career and instead moved to Copenhagen to attend Copenhagen Business School. Before starting, he took on a sales job at Tree Mobile, where his unconventional, creative techniques quickly made him one of Denmark's top salespeople. To draw attention to the shop, he wore a white t-shirt with a large box over his head, complete with eye holes, and attached demo phones. With "I'll give you a phone and a cheap subscription" written on his shirt, Mike wasn't scared to take a bold approach, and his survival instincts and natural flair for sales helped him thrive in a competitive environment.

"Your subconscious mind controls 90% of your life."

Mike quickly realised that whenever life pushed him to desperation, it didn't break him. Instead, it unlocked his most creative and successful side, revealing strengths he didn't know he had. When he took on the role of managing a local nightclub, he once again embraced his unconventional creativity, designing marketing campaigns that sparked excitement and attracted record-breaking crowds. He filmed guests enjoying themselves, creating an irresistible online buzz and introduced clever pricing strategies to fill the club on typically slow midweek nights. His growing reputation didn't go unnoticed, and soon a life-changing call came from the club's owner, who owned fifty-nine other venues across Denmark.

The owner invited Mike to Miami, offering him a glimpse of a life he had only ever dreamed of. Impressed by Mike's ingenuity, the owner invested 120,000 euros into Miinto, a business Mike had co-founded with his partner, Conrad. Today, Miinto has soared to generate 400 million euros in annual revenue, marking an extraordinary milestone in Mike's journey from humble beginnings to entrepreneurial success.

Nevertheless, before reaching this stage, Miinto took a significant toll on Mike's mental health. For four years, he lived in eight different countries, constantly on the move, boarding flights two to three times a week. The long, exhausting hours and relentless travel schedule eventually

"Diamonds are made under pressure."

> "An entrepreneur
> builds their wings on
> the way down."

pushed him to his breaking point. One day, while sitting on a flight, Mike had a "huge breakdown"—he couldn't remember where he was heading or where he'd come from. The stress and anxiety of his hectic lifestyle, combined with the loneliness of living in hotel rooms and the pressure to maintain the image of being "the strong one," became overwhelming.

So, when the opportunity arose to move to England and settle down, Mike seized it. He moved into a flat and, for the first time in years, resigned to stay in one place. No more flights or lonely hotel rooms—he began building a life with his girlfriend and finally found a sense of stability. However, this peace was short-lived when the UK operations were shut down, forcing him to relocate to Sweden to restructure the team, reducing it from thirty-five employees to just four. Looking back, Mike realises it wasn't the best decision, and soon after, the board chose to centralise operations in Denmark, rendering his efforts in Sweden unnecessary. The emotional and mental strain during this period was another key turning point in his life, and Mike ultimately decided to resign.

Encountering another low point, Mike once again tapped into his creativity and resilience and began developing a "Netflix-style business model for fitness influencers." The idea was simple but innovative: customers could subscribe to specific health and fitness influencers and receive personalised content, including diet plans and fitness routines, delivered as PDFs. This concept eventually evolved into Playbook Technologies, an app that quickly gained traction and resonated with a growing audience.

Despite the app's success, Mike's personal life remained plagued by the toll of his intense work lifestyle. He was still burdened by massive debt from his time at Miinto, and the pressure to pay it off weighed heavily on him. Frequent panic attacks and anxiety continued to overwhelm him, and after just four months of running Playbook Technologies, the stress became unbearable. Mike made the difficult decision to step down and move back to Sweden, choosing to prioritise his mental health over the success of the business.

Nevertheless, it was during his time in Sweden that Mike encountered his next stroke of fortune. At the last minute, he secured an investor for Miinto, allowing him to finally free himself from the crushing debt that had weighed on him for so long. The relief of resolving his financial struggles allowed him the space to recover from the anxiety and stress that had consumed him for years. For the first time in a long while, Mike could breathe again.

After the success of Playbook Technologies and overcoming his personal challenges, Mike launched another entrepreneurial venture in Sweden by founding Ocast. In just four years, he grew the company from twenty customers to around 400. However, Mike acknowledges that Ocast wasn't a venture born from passion but a necessity-driven venture, so after four years, he ultimately decided to resign.

Feeling the need for something more fulfilling than a money-making venture, Mike returned to his lifelong passion: fitness. He launched an Instagram account called 'toobusytobefit,' where he shared his fitness routines and lifestyle habits. The account quickly gained an audience, skyrocketing from 2,000 to 45,000 followers in a short time. Mike leveraged this platform to create an eight- and four--week online course aimed at helping employees become more energetic, motivated, and healthy. This new fitness venture proved wildly successful, generating 1.5 million euros in its first year.

> "We won't grow bigger than our belief in ourselves."

After years of struggle and trial and error, Mike is now an author and motivational speaker dedicated to helping others cultivate determination and a positive mindset. He recognised that while many people purchased his diet plans and training schedules, what was often lacking was the discipline and commitment to follow through. This realisation inspired him to launch his mentoring business, where he coaches people in structure, goal setting, and overcoming limiting beliefs. Additionally, he authored a book titled *Above Average*, aimed at guiding people to become the best version of themselves.

Mike's innovative spirit and fearless approach have not only defined his own path but have also motivated those around him to confront challenges head-on instead of succumbing to them. By sharing his experiences and insights, Mike illustrates that setbacks can serve as stepping stones to success, empowering people across the globe to embrace resilience and pursue their dreams with unwavering determination.

"The law of the mind is that
we can only act and behave
as we believe we are."

HOW TO
SURVIVE
AND
THRIVE
VOLUME II

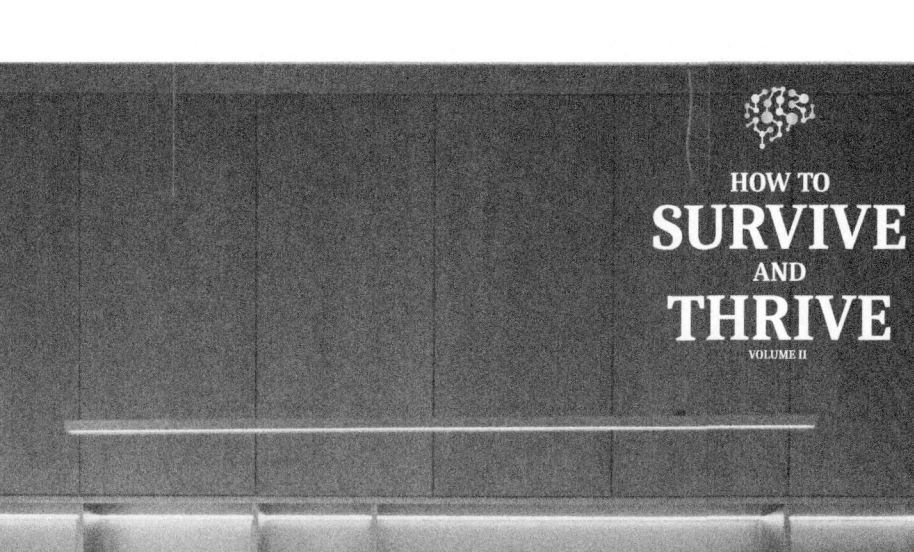

CHRIS BROWNE
Retail Expert

Chris Browne

As businessmen, Chris and I share a lot in common. We're both old school, favouring hands-on involvement on the shop floor, valuing the input of our teams, always remaining attentive to our customers' requirements, and travelling extensively to keep our global brands ahead of the competition, ultimately turning them into iconic household names. It's always enlightening to exchange insights with peers who have navigated similar challenges as I did at Reebok, learning from their triumphs and setbacks.

It's fair to say that Chris has had some setbacks, or rather survival moments, but for the most part, his stellar career has been a story of how to thrive in business.

Chris Browne attributes his success to his hyperactivity. Growing up in Worthing, Sussex, he always had an abundance of energy for both life and business. His entrepreneurial spirit emerged at just five years old when he would buy sweets from the corner shop and sell them to his brothers when the shop was closed.

His first job was as a newspaper boy, but he quickly grew tired of the cold and wet autumns. Instead, he persuaded the newsagent to let him mark up the papers while someone else did the rounds. This experience was a valuable lesson for Chris. He explains, "It was my earliest memory of entrepreneurship, realising there is a better way of doing things. If you think like that, you are likely to get elevated. You are likely to be the one running things."

> "It's about hard work, tenacity, standards, cleaning, and taking pride in your work."

With such an abundance of energy, one job just wasn't enough. Alongside his newspaper round, he worked in a pet store, where he discovered his passion for customer service, enjoying the direct interaction with the public and seeing how his efforts translated into sales. By the time he was seventeen, Chris had gained solid work experience in a newsagent, a pet store, and a bank. These early jobs laid the foundation for his future career in retail.

Nevertheless, school was challenging for the hyperactive teenage Chris, who was easily distracted. At twelve, he was nearly expelled for "causing trouble and coming up with crazy ideas to disrupt my classmates, like organising everyone to tip their powder paint on the floor on command." Yet Chris also displayed early signs of leadership and creativity. He started a school competition to build things out of twigs and sticks, with categories such as "best ranch," "best farm," and "best schoolhouse." Demonstrating his knack for organisation, he set up the event and also judged the entries, showcasing his early entrepreneurial spirit and leadership skills.

After leaving school, Chris began working in a shoe shop in Brighton. Living in a flat with very little money, he once found himself down to his last pennies and decided to buy an ice lolly. As he sat savouring it on the seafront, he realised he wasn't really moving forward in life. It was a pivotal moment, and within days, he resigned from his job, left his small flat in Brighton, and moved to London, where he found work on King's Road.

"Develop great people and train great people."

For someone in their early twenties during the eighties, London was buzzing with "clubs and distractions," but Chris remained focused on his job. One of his fondest memories was having Princess Diana as a regular customer; she often popped in after dropping off William and Harry at their nearby school.

Lessons were also learned, and Chris recounts how he spent much of his own money decorating the basement, only to be chastised by the boss. Today, he observes how shabby many retail spaces have become, noting that people no longer keep their work environments clean and tidy. He emphasises that "taking pride in your work is absolutely vital."

As a natural leader, Chris faced difficult decisions, such as letting go of about eight of his ten assistants who worked in the shop because "they didn't work hard and didn't try to sell." This taught him a valuable lesson: "Surround yourself with great people because you can't do these jobs on your own."

Chris was promoted to Sales Manager within six months because of his success in the King's Road store. He learned another valuable lesson: "If you do more than you are asked, the chances are you're going to be ahead of your competition and get rewarded." Chris did get rewarded, leading 3000 employees through the Ted Baker stores. He suggests that "with a repeatable

309

pattern and a standard and discipline to work to," working on a global basis is not as tough as it may seem.

As a seasoned retailer, Chris finds that one of his favourite things about running a business is asking new employees what they would bring to the company. He acknowledges that, even now, he is still learning and that lessons often come from the most unexpected sources. Chris explains how he became "obsessed with finding ideas and innovation from books, people, experiences, and brainstorming with my teams." This obsession led to creating "a fantastic retail bible called the School of Excellence," which compiles the valuable tips and lessons he has gathered from his travels and experiences.

For example, one Saturday morning, Chris walked into a Ted Baker store in Manchester and was immediately struck by the exquisite scent that filled the space. Intrigued, he sought out the source and discovered it was from a young woman who had just visited The Body Shop and accidentally spilled essential oils over herself. Inspired by this, Chris had the idea to position scented burners at the entrance of every Ted Baker store to create a welcoming atmosphere when customers walked in.

On another occasion, he visited a clothing company in Glasgow and was guided through the store by a seventeen-year-old employee. Chris found the teenager's use of language to describe the clothes captivating. He described the linen fabric as "soft as butter" and the trousers as "triple-stitched." It wasn't just the descriptive language but the young man's infectious enthusiasm and genuine excitement about the product that left a lasting impression.

Reflecting on his years in retail, Chris acknowledges that despite many successes, he also faced his share of failures. He recalls seasons when stores were filled with brown shirts, anticipating a trend that never materialised. To address this, he devised a clever merchandising strategy called 'Hide the Brown,' where he paired the brown items with white t-shirts or blue jumpers to break up the monotony. Additionally, he began referring to 'colour' as 'accent' when speaking with customers, a tactic designed to convince them that brown was the season's must-have hue.

Chris's playful spirit from his school days still shines through in his work. He recounts a memorable April Fool's prank when Ted Baker was threatened with a takeover by 'Country Casual' menswear. To lift the staff's spirits, he changed all store signs to

Country Casuals for the day. Another April Fool's joke involved shirts made in Hong Kong that fell foul of trading standards. Chris relabelled them with a code reading, 'April 1st—you've been had,' adding a touch of humour to the situation.

Behind the humour lies a steely determination and an unwavering work ethic. During his tenure at Ted Baker, Chris committed to spending 90% of his time in the stores. This dedication often meant starting his day before 5 a.m. and embarking on long journeys to various locations. He made it a point to arrive before the staff and leave after them, with some trips stretching to eight hours there and back, returning home well past midnight to begin anew the following day. Chris firmly believes, "The boss puts in the extra hours, and if you don't, you won't succeed."

Despite his relentless efforts, there were times when Chris feared the business might collapse. Yet, he pressed on, driven by a commitment to learn, adapt, and maintain a personal discipline he describes as "lean and mean." His enduring positive outlook, a quality he attributes to his mother, was crucial during these challenging periods. Chris considers his mother his greatest influence, crediting her steadfast optimism and "simple home-spun wisdom" in shaping his approach to business and life. As he often says, "I'm someone who thrives."

This optimistic mindset proved crucial as

the brand faced challenges establishing itself in the US Initially, the business struggled and lost money for four years, making success seem distant. Chris quickly pinpointed the core issue: the locations of their stores. By leasing and meticulously designing new outlets in San Francisco and Las Vegas, he turned the situation around by creating beautifully designed, welcoming stores that reflected the Ted Baker brand. These revitalised locations began to perform exceptionally well, reaffirming his belief in the power of perseverance and strategic adjustments.

At that time, the founder insisted on a boutique merchandising approach, which was very minimal and high-end. When Chris arrived, he quickly realised this strategy was ill-suited for Las Vegas, where customers were prone to impulse buying and spending freely. Trusting his instincts and going against his boss' directive, who was personally wedded to the idea of sparse shops with expensive merchandise, Chris overstocked the store and adopted a more commercial strategy. This shift created a dynamic new atmosphere that tripled the store's turnover within the first week.

With Chris' business acumen, creativity, and positive attitude, he found it easy to thrive in America. He recalls a memorable encounter when Ted Baker was preparing to open a store in a prestigious mall in Dallas. The leasing manager asked if Chris would meet "a gentleman from a computer company," who turned out to be Steve Jobs. Jobs was eager to meet the man behind Ted Baker Retail and complimented Chris on the business. This initial meeting marked the beginning of a notable alliance, as when Apple opened its first European store on Regent Street, they chose Ted Baker as a co-tenant.

As a seasoned retail professional, Chris is a strong advocate for the power of networking. He believes it's all too easy for people to "hide behind emails and team calls" and insists that the key to thriving in business is to "get out among the people in the industry." Attending events and conferences, even those that seem peripheral, can be invaluable. It's often in these settings that you make the connections that can truly propel your career and your brand forward.

Chris reflects on how much the business world has changed and maintains an old-school philosophy. He believes that "youngsters don't learn by being handed everything they want." His approach is straightforward: "If you don't meet my standards, don't work here. If you're unhappy with the job, find somewhere else. And if you keep calling in sick, this isn't the right place for you."

"Being tough is a good thing, be tough, but be tough with a purpose."

However, Chris also recognises the value of fostering a "culture of togetherness and teamwork" and emphasises the importance of bonding exercises and training events in achieving this. "You need to engage with people's lives, offer tough love when necessary, and be prepared to lead your team to success," he asserts.

He firmly believes that maintaining high standards of conduct and behaviour is crucial, and this commitment to excellence is deeply rooted in his passion for the brand. "I wanted to create a vibrant, fun, and welcoming environment where our teams would make every visitor feel valued and at home," he explains.

Chris's leadership philosophy highlights a critical issue with modern practices, where people often step into CEO roles without the requisite experience. He underscores the importance of effective communication in leadership, a lesson he learned first-hand while managing staff during a period of cash flow challenges. "There's a delicate balance between honesty and transparency," he explains. "It's crucial to share enough information so that employees don't feel deceived while also maintaining a strategic level of discretion. Mastering this balance is one of the greatest challenges in leadership."

Chris values straightforwardness and "truth-telling" in leadership. His advice is to "be candid and unafraid of being disliked; through this honesty, you will earn respect and a reputation for getting things done." For Chris, getting things done involves being hands-on and present, whether on the shop floor, in the stockrooms, or out in the field. He emphasises the importance of listening to the teams, capturing the voice of the customer, and then bringing those insights back to the office.

Chris's approach at Ted Baker exemplifies his hands-on philosophy. Initially, the collars on their shirts were quite stiff, a feature customers appreciated for keeping their ties in place. However, feedback revealed a demand for something more relaxed for summer wear. In response, Ted Baker introduced the casual collar, a softer option designed to meet customer needs. This change highlights Chris's commitment to listening and adapting based on customer input.

Chris extends this attentiveness to his team as well. He remembers fighting the whole board to be allowed to introduce the newly launched shoe range into stores, which had been intended for wholesale only. This decision ended up having a huge impact, not just on sales but also proving his theory that Ted Baker could be more than just a 'shirt store.' Chris also innovated with visual merchandising tricks and allowed store teams to localise their styling and presentation if they could justify the sales. Whilst this tactic didn't always run smoothly, it was a fun and inspirational way to engage teams working on the shop floor to feel part of the decision-making rather than just following directives.

Chris is eager to impart the valuable lessons he has accumulated over his decades in retail. These lessons include the importance of hard work, taking pride in your work, listening to everyone from young shop assistants to customers and CEOs, and maintaining a positive mindset. However, his most crucial piece of advice is aimed at those in leadership positions, "Never assume that you have all the answers just because you're behind a desk. To truly lead, you must get out there and listen to your teams."

"Stick to your guns even if you are a lone voice sometimes."

"Those who succeed tend to be the ones that put the most effort in."

HOW TO SURVIVE AND THRIVE

VOLUME II

MANNY OHONME

Chairman of Sanford Health World Clinics,
Founder and CEO of Samaritans Feet and World Shoe, Inc.

Manny Ohonme

As the Founder and President of World Shoe and Samaritan's Feet, Manny and I have a clear connection, yet his journey is nothing short of remarkable. With the constant love and support of his devoted mother, an unwavering faith, and a touch of serendipity, Manny learned to dream big—an attitude to life and business that I will always admire.

Growing up in Nigeria as the fourth child in a struggling family, Manny was no stranger to hard work, and by the age of nine, he had already become a street vendor. After school, he would grab his basket of drinks and head to the local park, where the sweltering African sun ensured plenty of thirsty customers.

One day at the park, he spotted a group of American aid workers teaching a group of children how to play basketball and found a way to sneak in and join the fun. Later that afternoon, one of the aid workers announced a competition with the grand prize being a brand-new pair of tennis shoes. By today's standards, the prize may seem a bit underwhelming, but for Manny, who lived in a country where shoes were a luxury only afforded by the rich, it felt like he was being given the chance to "win a Mercedes-Benz."

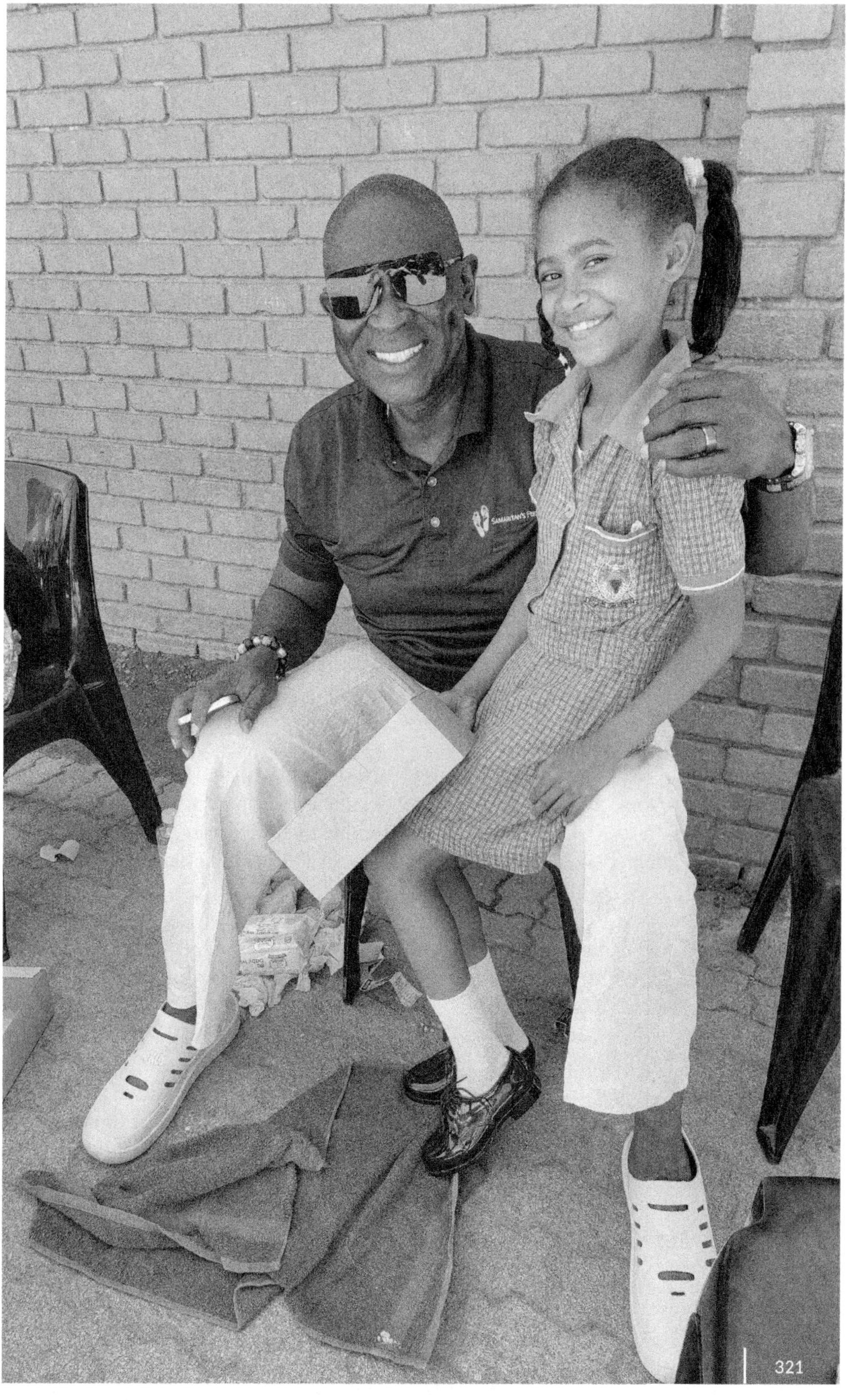

The task was simple: whoever could make the most shots won, and Manny, with focus and natural talent, took first place. It may not seem like much in today's world, but in Lagos at that time, it was a huge deal. Manny became the first person in his community to own a pair of tennis shoes—a moment of pride and achievement that has left a lasting impact.

That day, Manny won more than a pair of tennis shoes; he gained self-belief. As he was awarded the shoes, the aid worker told him to "Keep dreaming, and keep dreaming big," and that's exactly what he did.

The aid workers began holding regular basketball coaching sessions for the local kids, and Manny quickly fell in love with the sport. But life at home was difficult. His father, often drunk, would come home angry, leading to loud arguments and beatings. It was his mother who kept him grounded, always offering words of encouragement. "She reminded me constantly that I was created for a purpose, something much bigger," he explains.

Manny vividly remembers when his mother called him over to the window and asked, "What do you see?" He replied, "Trees." When she asked him to look higher, he saw the birds. "Look even higher," she urged, and finally, he saw the vast sky. Then she asked, "Why do you think the sky is so high?" Manny shook his head, unsure. "So poor boys like you can dream really high," she said. "Never make excuses. Just because today is bad, that doesn't mean tomorrow will be the same."

Her words remained in his heart and fuelling his determination. Manny worked hard at school and devoted himself to basketball, spending every spare moment honing his skills. After his junior year in high school, he approached his coach and mentor, sharing his dream of playing basketball in America. The coach replied honestly, "You're not fast enough and you're not big enough, but what you do have is courage." And it was Manny's courage, alongside his mother's wise words, that pushed him to dream big and succeed.

The coach gave Manny a list of schools in the US that he could apply to, with a warning that he should prepare himself for no response. On the contrary, Manny was offered five scholarships, and he eventually chose the University of North Dakota, Lake Region, mainly because of its appealing brochure. But getting a scholarship was only the first hurdle in Manny's journey to America.

He explains how his mother "sold everything she had. She worked and worked, borrowed and borrowed," until, somehow, from nothing, she eventually scraped together the $700 needed for his one-way plane ticket to the US Although a significant breakthrough, he still had more challenges to overcome before being able to realise his dream.

Manny's visa to enter the US was denied. Desperate, they turned to his uncle, a former member of the Nigerian military, who wrote a letter to the Embassy, vouching for his nephew. Armed with his passport and the letter, Manny returned to the Embassy, and this time, his visa was granted.

Finally, Manny boarded his first-ever flight, and unsure of how things worked; he didn't touch the in-flight food, thinking it would cost him extra. After landing in Rome, exhausted and hungry, he waited for his connecting flight to Chicago. With only $300 in his pocket, an amount that was meant to last him three years, he was anxious about every dollar.

"Education is key."

Upon arriving in Chicago, he discovered that he still needed to take another flight to reach his final destination in North Dakota. That unplanned expense ate into his precious budget, costing him $180—over half of his remaining money.

Manny hadn't thought to call ahead when he landed in North Dakota, so when he

"When you love the world, you want to leave it in a better place."

arrived at the airport, no one was waiting for him. With no plan and nowhere to go, he spent his very first night on the airport floor. The following day, determined to make it to the university, Manny decided to walk. With two heavy bags in tow and dressed for the warm weather back in Lagos, he began the two-kilometre trek in the cold, unfamiliar air of early winter.

However, as luck would have it, on their way back from church, a couple named Sheila and Larry spotted him struggling along the roadside and took him back to their home for a hot meal. For Manny, who had eaten very little since leaving Nigeria, the dinner of mashed potatoes, turkey, and stuffing was unlike anything he'd ever experienced before. It was also his first real introduction to the welcoming spirit of the community he would soon call home.

After Sheila and Larry dropped him off at the university, Manny was shown to his room. He was immediately struck by the sight of snow—his first experience with the "white stuff outside the window." The sight of it made him feel cold, and after a long internal debate, Manny decided to stay in a discontinued boiler room with no windows, where the constant warmth reminded him of Africa.

For two months, Manny didn't venture outside as he hadn't yet adjusted to the frigid temperatures. But when he did, he finally began playing basketball and meeting other students. His efforts paid off in more ways than one. In just two years, he graduated with a diploma in Liberal Arts and Agri-Business Management and was the first African to be crowned homecoming king at the University of North Dakota, Lake Region. By his side was his future wife, Tracy, who had been crowned homecoming queen. This new chapter marked a turning point in his life, both on and off the court.

Manny recalls how, back in Nigeria, he "would admit it's okay not to have breakfast, and maybe sometimes not to have lunch, but I would pray to God to at least let me have supper, so I could wake up the next day." These early experiences with hunger instilled in him a profound determination to alleviate some of the hardships children experience in the developing world.

Driven by this mission, he immersed himself in learning everything he could about agriculture, business, and supply chains. His goal was to eventually run the world's largest food agency, an ambition that was supported by the President of Concordia College in Minnesota, who recognised Manny's potential and offered him a full scholarship to study for a BA in International Relations and Business.

Afterwards, he continued his academic journey at North Dakota State University, where he earned an M.Sc. in Applied Economics. These achievements laid the groundwork for his future endeavours, equipping him with the skills and knowledge to make a meaningful impact.

As one of the top three students in his program nationally, Manny received an invitation to a prestigious conference in San Diego, California, where he had the opportunity to meet leading supply chain executives. This exposure led to a job offer from a technology company, and after a few years, he moved to a New York-based firm, fulfilling his aspirations whilst also "living the dream."

However, the death of his father prompted Manny to return to Nigeria, setting off a chain of events that would alter his path. Upon his return to Lagos, he was struck by the sight of children in the park, many of whom were barefoot and seemed devoid of hope. It reminded him of his own childhood and the aid worker who had inspired him to dream big.

Manny was shocked to learn that over 600 million people in Africa went without shoes, and there were tropical diseases transmitted through soil, as a direct result of being barefoot. Although this revelation was profound for Manny, at that time, he admits he was "too comfortable" with his executive role to give it all up and dedicate himself to charity work.

However, while he was working in his third software company, things started to shift. At an NBA game, his boss, Jay Rollins, asked him an out-of-the-blue question, "If money wasn't an issue, how would you change the world?" Manny knew the answer immediately but wondered why he was asked the question. Nevertheless, he told Jay that he'd provide shoes for children around the world. The conversation brought his idea to the forefront again, but he was still reticent to take the leap.

Shortly after that conversation, Tracy attended a conference where a woman unexpectedly pulled her aside with a message that felt both strange and prophetic. Manny recalls, "She told Tracy, 'You don't know me, and this might sound odd, but God has called you and your husband to a big vision—yet you keep putting God in a box.'" The woman briefly stepped away and returned with a bottle of water, offering to wash Tracy's feet.

What made the moment even more surreal was its timing. Manny and Tracy had just begun planning their charity work, which included a unique step: washing children's feet before giving them new shoes. This detail, known only to the two of them, was essential to their vision, reflecting the charity's Christian roots—humility and dignity, alongside the importance of cleanliness to prevent disease. Tracy's unexpected encounter deepened the spiritual significance of their mission, reinforcing

"Every choice has a consequence."

the couple's commitment to pursuing their vision of helping children in need. They felt a clear sense of divine confirmation. Yet, despite this powerful affirmation, Manny still hesitated, feeling the weight of responsibility for his mother and siblings in Nigeria, and unsure if he could fully embrace such uncertainty.

Manny believes God played a role in guiding him towards his big decision. Just days after grappling with his uncertainty, he received news that his company was being taken over, leading to the loss of his job. Initially, he thought it would be the worst day of his life. But with time, he began to see it differently. Losing his job became a blessing in disguise, freeing him from the constraints of corporate life and giving him the opportunity to pursue his true passion: helping others. This pivotal moment set him on a new path, ultimately leading him to dedicate his life to providing shoes and hope to children around the world while also teaching them the importance of hygiene.

Since founding Samaritan's Feet in 2003, the organisation has provided over 11 million pairs of shoes to people in need across 111 countries and 625 cities in the United States. Most of these shoes come from "the West: North America, Europe, and sometimes Asia," but Manny wanted to go further. His vision was to "empower Africans to have the solutions in their hands." This led him to create

"Every human being on earth has the right to an education."

a social enterprise that generates jobs, fosters economic development, and expands opportunities. The result was The World Shoe factory in Ghana, which produces five million antimicrobial, biodegradable, and sustainable shoes annually.

Manny has rallied athletes, coaches, TV personalities, pastors, governors, corporate executives, and even heads of state worldwide to join the cause, raising awareness for Samaritan's Feet by going barefoot in solidarity with children in need. Notably, South Africa's Springbok Sevens rugby team once went barefoot to receive their world champion trophies. Major networks and news outlets, including ESPN, FOX, NBC, CBS, PBS, NBA, and NFL, have covered this impactful barefoot movement.

Since its founding, some of Samaritan's Feet's shoe recipients have gone on to become police officers, doctors, nurses, government officials, business leaders, and even professional athletes in the NBA and NFL. As Manny explains, "Samaritan's Feet's mission is to inspire H.O.P.E.: Health, Opportunity, Peace, and Education."

Manny has also recently launched *The World Shoe*, a groundbreaking footwear brand designed to be marketed and sold across Africa and globally. The brand's mission is to fund his philanthropic initiatives while making a lasting impact. With the support of his dedicated team, Manny has established a state-of-the-art factory in Akosombo, Ghana, where they produce shoes equipped with built-in antimicrobial properties to fight diseases and prevent injuries. The shoes also feature an eco-friendly additive that accelerates biodegradation, positioning them among the most sustainable footwear options in the world. Manny's ultimate goal is to create a world where no one is without shoes, and until that vision is realised, he has no plans of slowing down.

It took five years from Manny's initial concept to realising his dream of helping the world walk in shoes. During that time, he witnessed the transformative power of faith. It was then that he fully understood his mother's words—that he was created for a greater purpose, something far beyond himself.

"Service to others
emancipates humanity
from the dungeon of self."

HOW TO
SURVIVE
AND
THRIVE
VOLUME II

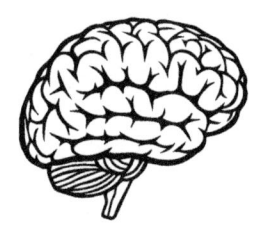

"Never underestimate who you're talking to because they could end up being your next business partner, your next joint venture partner, your potential client or friend."

Tracey Currell
Director and Founder of Introbiz

"You don't get what you deserve.
You get what you expect."

Sherrika Sanders
Founder of Transform the GAAP

"Talk more about money. The conversation will help you learn more about who you are, what's most important to you, what you value, how you feel, and what your purpose is in life."

Sandi Bragar
CCO of Aspirant

"Don't start out trying to sell. Don't start out with a product. Start with empathy for your customer. If you do that, you will always be starting from the right place."

Scott Robertson
Founder of Robertson Communications

"Business is something that you can learn in the process. Think, ask, strategise, work, and repeat."

Shahid Hussain
Founder and CEO of Green Proposition

"We don't live in a real world. We live in a construct. This is liberating because if you live in the real world and you don't like it, you're screwed. But if you live in a construct and you don't like it, you can deconstruct the parts of it that don't fit you and you can build it up again."

Srikumar Rao
Coach

"If you have nothing, you have a competitive advantage. If you have too much, it might be holding you back."

Simon Squibb
Investor and Founder of HelpBnk

"Don't waste your time craving the unobtainable. Chase the obtainable."

Stian Rognlid
CEO of Aquaticode

"Saving an animal doesn't change the world, but it changes the world for that animal. If you're able to give this gift to another living being, you too will be forever changed."

Stephen Quandt
Feline Training and Behaviour Specialist

"No free and fair union of equals can last without a shared purpose and vision. That system has to be organised structurally."

Stan Tatkin
Author and Researcher

"Manage your energy, don't waste it, and don't let people rob you of it."

Stuart Jackson
CEO of ICE Creates

"When something goes wrong, let yourself have twenty-four hours and then take a risk to counteract the negativity. Nine times out of ten, it will bring something really unusual and special."

Lauretta and Sharon, the Gavin Sisters
Founders of The Detox Barn

"The mission of business is to help people."

Will Adams
President of Tarkenton

"People think that entrepreneurship is like lightning striking, but it's actually a science. It's a sequence of understanding events to make sure that you are very, very unlikely to build something that no one wants."

Tom Ferguson
Founder of Burnt Island Ventures

"Survival can feel as though your life is full of suckers, whereas boosters are the people, places, activities, and things that fill up your energy stores and make you feel great. Thriving will feel as though your life is full of boosters. Balance your life by consciously adding boosters."

Vanda North
Change-maker at The Change Maker Group

"For a human-centered leadership approach, treat others how you wish to be treated."

Vicky Hampson
Founder of DEFY EXPECTATIONS

"Lean into your discomfort to discover what doesn't align with what you want to do. Things that make you uncomfortable signal where you can grow in your career and personal life."

William Watson
Senior Engineer at MDA Space

"In the fast-paced world of business, curiosity is a superpower. By supporting curiosity, companies tap into the collective intelligence of their workforce, fuelling a continuous cycle of learning, adaptation, and growth."

William J. Ryan
Founder of Ryan Consulting, LLC

"Trust your authentic voice and intuition to guide your evolution."

Yetunde Shorters
Purposeful Personal Branding Coach

"Follow your dreams no matter what because you never know what will happen. If your dreams are genuine, then they may come true."

Zoltan Vigh
Business Leader and Consultant

Spotlight Nugget

"Take the time you need to make the best decision. Be willing to step back and press pause so you have the time and space to evaluate the data, speak with your team, and think things through."

Ellen Williams
CEO of The Salient Strategist

GRATITUDE

I am deeply grateful to all the co-authors who have joined us on this incredible journey—each of you has been a true source of inspiration. My heartfelt thanks to the amazing team at One Golden Nugget: Greta, Anna, David, Maxwell, Trevor, and Steven—your dedication and creativity have been invaluable. And to my wife, Julie, who is the heart and driving force behind everything I do—thank you for being my unwavering support.

Joe Foster
Founder of Reebok

Printed in Great Britain
by Amazon